PURITAN SPIRITUALITY

Irvonwy Morgan

PURITAN SPIRITUALITY

Illustrated from the Life and Times of the Rev. Dr JOHN PRESTON, Master of Emmanuel College, Cambridge; Town Preacher of Cambridge; Preacher at Lincoln's Inn; Chaplain to Prince Charles: Adviser to George Villiers, Duke of Buckingham; Leader of the Jacobean Puritan Movement.

London

EPWORTH PRESS

First published in 1973
by Epworth Press

Enquiries should be addressed to
The Methodist Publishing House
The Book Room
2 Chester House, Pages Lane
London N10 1PZ

Printed in Great Britain by
The Garden City Press Limited
Letchworth, Hertfordshire SG6 1JS

7612 0227 1

Contents

ONE

The Foolishness of Preaching

'Now in the time of the Gospel, God had appointed the foolishness of preaching, for so the world accounts it to be, the means whereby He will save those that believe.' So spake Lord Saye in a parliamentary speech on 22nd February 1642. The foolishness of preaching! Lord Saye could not have summed up the dynamic that underlay the Puritan movement more adequately, for Puritanism in the last resort must be assessed in terms of the pulpit. The Puritan clergy were preachers first and everything else second.[1]

In the early days of Elizabeth I, when after the turmoil of the two previous reigns, the Church in England settled down to what Archbishop Parker called 'a reverent mediocrity' in worship summed up in *The Book of Common Prayer*, the amount of preaching in the church was small.

In mediaeval times much of the preaching was done by the religious orders, particularly the great preaching orders of the Dominicans and Franciscans, but nearly every monastery had parish churches on their land, from which they drew the tithes, maintaining from part of the tithes the priest to serve the church and supplying the preachers themselves. At the time of the Dissolution of the monasteries in the days of Henry VIII, about a third of the land was owned by the monastic orders. This whole region of the Church's life was wiped out in a few years and about two-fifths of the advowsons of the Church reverted to the Crown or to lay impropriators and with them also the rights of presentation to the livings. The importance of this change in

[1] Irvonwy Morgan, *The Godly Preachers of the Elizabethan Church*, p. 11.

respect of the life of the Church was that the urge to produce preachers was consequently diminished.

But concern for a preaching ministry was kept alive throughout the long reign of Elizabeth I by clergymen who were convinced that one of the first, and in some cases the only, call was to be preachers of the Word of God. By the end of Elizabeth's reign they formed a distinct group within the Church with an ethos and a purpose of their own. They met in conferences and what were called 'prophesyings' which were preaching exercises with the purpose of training preachers themselves, and through these means aimed at the conversion of individuals and the exercising of spiritual discipline in the lives of their converts. Many of them only found a living in the Church by becoming 'Lecturers' in parish churches, paid for by the congregation or by some patron with Puritan sentiments or, in some cases, by borough councils. But by the early years of the seventeenth century, though numerically small, they were a powerful and articulate body with the ear of influential lords and squires, lawyers and business men, in Parliament, in the Inns of Court, and in corporate towns. They were not popular with the Establishment at Court, because they had the ear of the people, who flocked to hear their sermons, but they had a sufficient number of prominent patrons in the Lords and Commons to enable them to get by without too much trouble when one of their number was suspended from preaching for some reason or other. John Preston came to the leadership of this movement in the reign of James I, and the first sermons published after his untimely death in 1628 were dedicated to his great friend Lord Saye, and to Lord Saye's son-in-law, the Earl of Lincoln, who had been Preston's pupil at Cambridge. Subsequent collections of sermons were dedicated to the Earls of Warwick, Bedford, and Pembroke, Lord Brook, Lady Vere, Sir Richard Knightly, Nathaniel Rich, John Pym and Henry Lawrence, most of whom were his intimate friends. This is a nominal roll of the Puritan opposition of the Jacobean period and indicates the respect in which John Preston was held by the political men of the Puritan Movement.

The energy displayed in prosecuting the importance of preaching by the Godly Preachers, as they were called, had its correlative in the growth of congregations who desired a preaching ministry. Nehemiah Wallington, a small shopkeeper in Eastcheap, could record in his diary that as a young man in the 1620s he had in one week attended nineteen sermons, and this in the small compass of the City of London! When Preston came to the leadership of the Puritan Preachers, it was with the avowed purpose of increasing the scope and means of Puritan preaching. He was, says his biographer, determined to get places for himself, but with the aim of furthering the Puritan cause. He set himself with considerable political skill to reach the centre of power, namely, a place at Court, and in 1621, by the instance of James I's Favourite, the Duke of Buckingham, he was appointed Chaplain to Prince Charles.[2]

No other Puritan Preacher of his or the preceding generation of preachers attained such an important post. He attended the Prince every year during his term as Court Preacher and was present with the Prince and the Duke of Buckingham when James I died at his country palace 'Theobalds'. He travelled back to Whitehall in the same coach as the Prince and the Favourite, offering spiritual consolation now to this one, now to the other. Preston had a great affection for the Duke of Buckingham and was convinced at one time of the 'Saintship of the Duke'! His confidence in Buckingham waned towards the end of his life and the Puritan group in Parliament who had been guided by Preston and Lord Saye's leadership eventually abandoned the Duke and prosecuted his impeachment. But Preston held his Court appointment until the end of his life. During the short time of his influence at Court, from 1621–28, he succeeded in placing himself in many influential posts. In 1622 he was appointed Preacher at Lincolns Inn, from which so many members of Parliament were recruited. In 1622 he was made Master of one of the largest Cambridge Colleges, and the most Puritan, Emmanuel College. In 1623 he was made a Doctor of his University by Royal Mandate. In 1624 he fought a battle against the wishes of the King, the Arminian party, and the University authorities, to win the coveted post of Town Preacher of Cambridge. He was offered the Bishopric of Gloucester if he would withdraw his name, but he refused, for the 'Trinity Lecture', as it was called, outrivalled in popularity, both among undergraduates and

[2] Irvonwy Morgan, *Prince Charles's Puritan Chaplain*, ch. 4.

townsmen, the sermons preached at the University Church. He was even offered the Great Seal in an attempt to wean him away from his Puritan associates, but he again refused the bait.

Yet it would be a mistake to see John Preston merely as an able and intelligent man determined to prosecute his own career. He gave up thoughts of worldly advancement in business or in medicine when he was converted around 1611, by a sermon preached in the University Church by John Cotton. He was already a most successful tutor, reckoned to be one of the best philosophers in the University, and could have pursued a University career. But his conversion under the sermon turned him to divinity, which until that time he had considered to be a kind of 'honest silliness'. At one time during his friendship with the great Favourite it was said that he could have had any preferment he wanted in the Church, but the posts he sought and obtained were all preaching posts. He never deviated from his Puritan faith in the power and necessity of preaching to bring man to Christ and the nation to God.

Puritan preaching in its day had its own ethos, and the preachers are often called 'spiritual preachers' in contrast to the 'witty' preaching of so many Anglican divines. 'Witty' preaching was not necessarily theological preaching, it was what we may call 'clever' preaching, often lively, always scholarly, naturally metaphysical, full of quotations and allusions, and matched to the style of contemporary literary fashion. It drew on the Fathers of the Church for its inspiration, classical authors and contemporary humanism for its illustrations. It was, in the hands of a master, often dramatically emotional with a sophisticated wit popular at Court and University. But to the Puritan Preachers it conveyed what Samuel Clarke called 'the wisdom of words' rather than 'the words of wisdom'. It did not seem to them to treat the great issues of heaven and hell, salvation and damnation, Christ and Satan, holiness and sin with sufficient seriousness.

To confront men with these great themes was the purpose of the Godly Preachers. 'Now is the acceptable time, now is the day of salvation'[3] was their watchword. They were existentialist preachers, for salvation is to be known here and now in this life. There is a 'Kingdom of Grace', to use a phrase of John Preston's,

[3] John Preston, *The New Covenant* (1629), p. 190.

to which a man can belong now, and once he belongs to it he can never be robbed of it. If a man is not in the 'Kingdom of Grace', then he remains in the 'Kingdom of Destruction', predestinate to hell for eternity. This gave an urgency to their preaching, a passion for conversions and a terrible need for growing in grace in a life of holiness so that a man might be acceptable to God, who had delivered him from the 'Chambers of Death'. This urgency often communicated itself emotionally to the preachers, giving their sermons a sense of reality. One can hardly imagine any of the Court and University preachers of the days of Elizabeth or James being called 'the thundering preacher', but this was the name given to Peter Bulkly a friend of John Preston, who had to fly to America to escape Archbishop Laud's clutches. Oliver Heywood describes in *The Life of John Angier*, one of Preston's pupils, the people of Essex as saying, 'Let us go to Dedham to get a little fire!' John Rogers was the Lecturer there and Heywood describes him taking hold of the canopy of the pulpit and roaring hideously to represent the torments of the damned, which, says Heywood, 'had an awakening force attending it'. Another Lecturer at Dedham of a previous generation mourned in his diary when the Lord did not give him the grace of weeping in his sermons. All this passion, this urgency, this challenge was aimed at the conversion of souls. Preaching was the sword of the Spirit[4] which separated the elect from the damned and 'every sermon which is heard', says Preston, 'sets us nearer Heaven or Hell'.[5]

Yet, though preachers were needed to labour men's conversion, conversion was not the act of the natural man choosing, as it were, between two courses of action. It was a supernatural act of God's Grace to those He willed to save, and worked in man by the Holy Spirit.

In the sermons published under the title *The Saint's Qualification* John Preston gives his own analysis of conversion, firstly, in ten sermons on the text, (Romans 1:18) which deals with the need for humiliation in men which must precede justification; secondly, in nine sermons on sanctification on the text (II Corinthians 5:17) which examines what it means to be a new

[4] John Preston, *The Saint's Qualification* (1637), p. 101.
[5] John Preston, *A Pattern of Wholesome Words*, p. 288.

creature in Christ. However, the sermons are not theological lectures which analyse the corrupt nature of man, the strivings of the Holy Spirit in the soul, the majesty of God's mercy to the repentant sinner, the Saint's reward in God's glory, as if these were theoretical propositions. These are sermons, evangelical sermons, aimed not just at analysing conversion but at persuading men to accept Christ as their Saviour. They are personal, persistent pleadings to men to see their corrupt state and accept the saving grace of Christ and save themselves from the wrath to come. 'Learn then', says the Preacher, 'to justify God and to condemn ourselves, to think well of Him, and ill of ourselves, to give Him the glory of His mercy, patience and long suffering, and to take shame to ourselves, and lay the blame where it ought to be laid';[6] on the other hand, 'If you will come in to Him, everything shall owe you a good turn. You shall look on nothing, but it is for you.... Let this move you then to come in; if you will not, however, you may live in this world and have some sweetness with them that have their portion in this life, yet they shall do you hurt, and in the latter end so you shall find it.'[7] To John Preston, as to all the Puritan Preachers, the end of preaching was not theological theorizing, but conversion and the saving of men's souls.

John Preston preached a series of sermons on preaching which were published thirty years after his death under the title *A Pattern of Wholesome Words*[8] (his translation of II Timothy 1:13). The sermons were obviously taken down as they were preached and later the full notes were pieced together to form a book. Unpolished as they are, they give us an insight into his thoughts on preaching and illustrate something of his style. His method of developing a sermon was very much on the question and answer pattern. It reminds one of the scholastic method of teaching, namely to state a point, raise one objection after another, answer the objections, and give reasons for so doing. His biographer, Thomas Ball, tells us that when Preston decided to become a preacher he turned his attention from medicine to theology, and read widely in the Fathers and, perhaps surprisingly

[6] *The Saint's Qualification*, p. 218.
[7] *The New Covenant*, p. 456.
[8] *A Pattern of Wholesome Words* (1658), p. 319.

for a son of the Reformation, in the Schoolmen, particularly St Thomas Aquinas and Duns Scotus. But as a good Puritan he studied what Ball calls the 'modern' authors, such as John Calvin, and Preston is at pains in his sermons to explain why Calvin was 'the best since the Apostles'. Even Augustine and the Fathers could not compare with him, for the Fathers spent their strength in particular controversies against Pelagius, Arius, and so on, so that their ability was concentrated in the cause they opposed, as 'when water runs strong in one channel it is weakened in another'. Calvin, however, was raised up to abolish Anti-Christ, namely the Pope, for whom the Fathers paved the way and thus turned the whole Church into heresy. So, if a Preacher was to use quotations at all, of which Preston was very doubtful, then 'modern' authors were better than the Fathers. Preston's style had been affeced by his studies in the Schoolmen, and their particular use of reason rather than exhortation gave to all his preaching and lecturing this rational basis, so that he was reputed among the Puritans to have a rational approach to theology.

Preaching, according to John Preston, is a public interpreting of the Word of God, performed by an Ambassador or Minister who speaks to people in the stead of God, and in the name of Christ. Preaching is a public act and not a private interpretation of the Word. Women may interpret privately but not publicly in the Church. They are forbidden by St Paul. Interpreting the Word, or dividing the Word means to collect some point out of the text and to support it by other texts lending to the proof or confirmation of it, 'For notions be scattered in Scripture as cards that are mingled, but when every suit is gathered and put together they make up a pair.'[9] The application is then made to 'particular persons of men'. The Minister is not a private man, he is commissioned to speak in Christ's name, 'the Apostles from Christ, and we from them'. The text must be grammatically analysed if necessary and the rhetorical analysis is added to explain the metaphor and figures in the text. The sense is then given and is confirmed from the scope of the text, the collection of other Scripture, and from the analogy of faith; dividing the Word is like 'giving a loaf of bread to children, the parts must be separated from the whole'. In confirming the text, reasons

[9] 'Riches of Mercy', *A Pattern of Wholesome Words*, p. 321.

will be given, for reasons increase a man's assent and make him yield the more.

In accordance with the Puritan method of preaching, every sermon had to have its use, that is, it must be applied to particular sins and dispositions of the heart. In order to illustrate this, Preston uses the idea of the Gospel being a medicine for the soul. 'Suppose', he says, 'a man have a desire like a feaver, an inflammation of lust, see what reasons the Word has against it and apply them in particular.'[10] He goes on to a medical description of other sins, such as 'a swelling of pride', a 'palsie of anger', a 'lethargy of idleness', a 'humour of vain glory', a 'plurasie of security', an 'unsavoury breath of evil speeches', all terms he had come across when he studied medicine at Cambridge, and he transposes them to delineate particular sins, each of which is examined in the light of what the Word of God says. 'This', he says, 'is a direction to the hearers of the Word of God to lead them to study the infallible Word, to meditate on its teaching and to apply this teaching to their own particular sins which will give them a sure salvation.'

It goes without saying that a sermon must conform to the Word of God. The Word must be presented in a spiritual manner, plain and unadorned, and easy to follow; preachers must not be like 'spiders merely spinning webs to show their skill'.[11] So what is delivered in preaching must be *per se credible*, and that by the primary authority in it felt, and not derived from others, for the 'Scripture receives no other witness but its own'. Yet for reasons of illustration it is permissible to quote other authors occasionally, for though all our weapons must be spiritual 'we may sharpen our weapons at the forge of Heathen writers'.[12] It is not however permissible to use the excellence of human learning in the testimonies of God. Human learning must be studied and absorbed, and 'as we feed our beasts with hay, we do not look for hay in return, but wool and milk', so human learning must be digested only that the understanding be strengthened.

The aim of the Preacher must be to preach sermons that are

[10] Ibid., p. 289.
[11] Ibid., p. 304.
[12] Ibid., p. 310.

'unadorned'. A Preacher may not gild his sermons to set them out better, for this only appeals to weak and flighty minds; 'weeds in corn adorn it to children, but wise men will account the worse of it'.[13]

The Preacher does not really need to go beyond Scripture where there are ample examples which he can use as illustrations. 'Why do we go' he asks, 'to the wide wastes to gather flowers, when the Scripture is our garden of Eden, it is true we may find violets by the way, so may we in common writers, and there is a choiceness in them, but nothing compared to the Scriptures.'[14]

He also has a word about the pastoral function of the Preacher. Just as it is best for mothers to suckle their own children, so the Preacher must feed his own flock, and this feeding must be done regularly, at least twice every Sabbath day. Preaching must be supplemented by catechising the people, in which the Preacher can temper the message to the understanding of the people. The Preacher's words must be pleasant and not such as people loathe, and he may bring a 'variety of dishes so that they be out of God's pantry'.[15] Yet the sermon must be methodically delivered and clearly divided. It was said that the walls of Byzantium were built of stones so closely formed that you would think it was one stone; 'this may be a commendation in a wall', says Preston, 'but not in a sermon.'[16] Nor may a Preacher attack true religion under the name of Puritan or precision, implying a hypocritical piety, for there are hypocrites everywhere, and those who made a show of piety, 'hanging out flags for it, as it were'. True religion, like a fire, must break forth and show itself; as the Spanish proverb says, 'Three things cannot be kept in, fire, love, and a man's cough'[17] and Preston adds the word 'grace' to these because true religion is the gift of God's grace to the elect and must be seen by the world.

He has words too, for hearers of the Word, for they have their part in the pattern of wholesome words. They will learn to discuss what is wholesome, by 'proving all things' and 'trying the

[13] Ibid., p. 319.
[14] Ibid., p. 320.
[15] Ibid., p. 302.
[16] Ibid., p. 302.
[17] Ibid., p. 313.

Spirit'. They must cultivate spiritual tastes and learn to distinguish between the pure Word and the 'froth of eloquence'. But, the most important discipline is to retain what they have heard and to do this by recalling and repeating the Word after it is delivered. Not to do this is to quench the Spirit for when He blows in our souls we must, like sailors setting sail when the wind blows, set our sails in the way to Heaven. Nor will this conferring on the Word after it is preached be abortive, for the 'Word is like Jonathan's bow, it never returns empty'.[18] His last word is to remind his audience that preaching the Word 'is of a masculine oratory', and that for men to be '*calamistrati et compti*' with excessive concern about their hair and appearance, effeminate and elegant in style detracts from the Word. What is needed is a plain, manly, clean exposition with the least adornment possible and the least distraction, either in appearance or expression from the pure milk of the Word of God.

As we have mentioned, the Godly Preachers of the Jacobean Church came to be called 'spiritual' preachers in contrast to the 'witty' preaching of the growing number of Arminian Divines.[19] Lancelot Andrewes, Bishop of Ely, was the doyen of this model of preaching which was popular at Court where a good sermon was as much appreciated as a good play. T. S. Eliot asserts that Andrewes was the first great preacher of the English Catholic Church,[20] but this somewhat tight definition tends however to beg the question, for it assumes that the English Church was 'Catholic' in the restrictive sense in which Eliot uses the word. From one aspect this is what the dispute between the Puritans and the Arminians was all about. Andrewes, however, was convinced that the English Church was 'Catholic', not Roman Catholic, for he was as certain as any Puritan that Rome had erred, and entered into controversy with the redoubtable Cardinal Bellarmin in defence of the English Church. Here he defined what was for him and his school, the Catholic Faith, 'For one Canon given by God, two testaments, three symbols, the first four councils, five centuries, and the series of Fathers there-

[18] Ibid., p. 288.
[19] William Haller, *The Rise of Puritanism*, p. 19.
[20] T. S. Eliot, *Selected Essays*, 'Lancelot Andrewes', p. 320.

in fix the rule of religion'.'[21] To the Puritans this definition of the Faith once delivered to the Saints was, at the least, illogical, for if the works of the Fathers of the Church in the first five centuries merely clarified what was implicit in the simplicity of the Gospel, why put a term of five centuries as the rule of religion? Why not fifteen centuries? The Puritans held not that the Fathers were orthodox but that the Papacy had erred, but that the Fathers had prepared the way for the Papacy and all its errors, and that the only sure way to know the Faith was by sticking to the Bible with its record and recollection of those who had met Christ and walked with Him, for they were bound to know the truth. St Paul was included among these witnesses since he had been met directly, and had been chosen for his Apostleship, by the risen Christ on the road to Damascus, and was personally directed by the Holy Spirit on his missionary journeys. As we shall see, 'spiritual' preaching was really the expounding of Pauline theology.

Andrewes himself had an astonishing knowledge of the Bible, equal to that of any of the finest Puritan Preachers. He also had a great dexterity in the use of the Text, both in its original language and its various versions and readings. But his knowledge was displayed in a wider setting than that used by the Preachers, for the Preachers rarely went outside the Bible for any support for their expositions. Richard Rogers, in his *Seven Treatises*, which were the sermon-lectures he had preached over the years, quotes hundreds of Scripture texts, but only once from Calvin and Peter Martyr, and from no one else. Whereas Andrewes quotes from Rabbinical writings, the Fathers, mediaeval writers, and pagan authors. His sermons, as those of all the Arminian Divines, are full of Latin and Greek and show an erudition unmatched even in his day. It was this erudition which appealed to King James, who was a considerable scholar himself. But, it was not only Andrewes' erudition and scholarly analysis of words and their meaning which marked his popularity as a Court Preacher, for he could, as T. S. Eliot says, 'Take a word and derive a world from it',[22] it was the way he expressed himself. His preaching was colloquial, almost casual, expressed with great charm

[21] Lancelot Andrewes, *Respons. Ad Bellarmin*, p. 26.
[22] T. S. Eliot, *Selected Essays*, p. 323.

and at times a facetious wit. He preached from very full notes, and this gave his vivid imagination an ease and flexibility of expression which used alliteration, onomatopoeia and assonance almost to pedantry. T. S. Eliot says that to read Andrewes' sermons on a theme like the Incarnation is like listening to a great Hellenist expounding a text of the *Posterior Analytics*, altering the punctuation, inserting a comma, dwelling on and analysing the various uses of a single word, purifying a cryptic lecture-note into lucid profundity.[23] As Canon Brightman says, 'It is clear from what was said of him as a preacher that his delivery was a real part of the charm of his sermon.'[24] His style however did not please everyone even at Court. One of the Scottish Lords told the King who had asked him how he liked Bishop Andrewes' sermons, that the Bishop was learned, 'but he did play with the Text, like a Jack-an-apes does, who takes up a thing and tosses and playes with it, and then he takes up another, and playes a little with it. Here's a pretty thing, and there's a pretty thing.'[25] The Scottish Lords at Court were the ones who were trying to get the Puritan Leader, John Preston, made a Court Preacher, and it was Puritan preaching which obviously appealed to these Calvinist Courtiers.

But, it was not merely the style and erudition of the preaching of Andrewes and the Arminian Divines to which the Puritans objected, it was to the whole philosophy of Christian Churchmanship which underlay their style. The philosophy which asserted that the English Church was Catholic, with all that it implied of ritualism, ceremonial and sacramental sacerdotalism. Andrewes and the Arminian Divines firmly believed that the Christian Church was a cultic organism, and they were the defenders and expounders of the cultic nature of the Church. 'Our religion', says Andrewes, 'and cultus must be uncovered, and a bare-faced religion';[26] and in his *A Discourse of Ceremonies* he frankly recognizes the pagan parallels and origins of Christian ceremonies. He was very conscious of the long historical background of the Church and of the way it had developed, by absorbing, re-orientating, and baptising into the Faith much of

23 Ibid.

24 F. E. Brightman, *The Preces Privatae* (Intro.) (1903), p. 30.

25 John Aubrey, *Brief Lives* (Ed. Anthony Powell), p. 166.

26 Serm. Temptation (v. p. 554).

the culture and cults of the Roman, Hellenistic, and pagan worlds. To Andrewes this syncretism was the inevitable consequence of a universalist religion, and merely supplied the true meaning to what the world had worshipped in ignorance. Religion was worship, and the focal point of this worship was where God had been traditionally thought of as objectively and substantially present in the congregation, namely, in the Sacrament of the Altar. Here was the demonstration of the Deity, the King of Kings, the Lord of Lords, present with His people. The recognition of the Lordship of God demanded not only spiritual insight but corporal worship in acts of devotion and actions which acknowledged the Presence, as one would acknowledge the presence of an earthly monarch, an analogy Andrewes was fond of expounding. This was exercised in an elaborate ceremonial which was faithfully carried out in his private chapel at Ely. There in the ceremonial surrounding the Presence, was reenacted the sacrifice of our Lord, which, by common consent was the source of saving grace. From this centre was conveyed sacramental grace through a ministry of apostolic succession and divine right, regenerating men in baptism, confirming them in the Faith by the imposition of priestly hands, imparting forgiveness by the power of the keys, and generally feeding their souls that they might bring forth the fruits of the Spirit. All else, even preaching, was subsidiary. If he preached twice in a day, said Andrewes, then one sermon was mere prating. As for the mysteries of election and predestination, he confessed in his *Judgement of the Lambeth Articles* that in his sixteen years as a priest he had never in public or private ventured to discuss predestination! Although he was a great and popular preacher, most certainly at Court, he considered that the age exaggerated the importance of preaching, and that the hearing of sermons was not the chief object of religious exercises. Preaching was an aid to worship, but was ineffective unless it stimulated devotion, and particularly devotion to the Eucharist. No wonder he and his school were charged with Popery! To the Puritans they seemed to betray not merely the Reformation, but the Gospel itself. To say that he thought so little of predestination, the heart of the Gospel, that he had never preached a sermon on it, appeared like a repudiation of the Articles of the English Church which were framed in a Calvinist mould and needed to be explained to the people. Andrewes' view on religion was that its essence was contemplation, so that even faith was a thing indifferent; any value it had arose from the object of faith, and the true approach to that object was reverent adoration in praise and prayer.

The Puritan Preachers, on the other hand, thought of religion as confrontation rather than contemplation, the confrontation of sinful man with a righteous God. There was no need to elaborate the preliminaries to the confrontation by mere distinctions in words and their meanings, or to confuse the issue by speaking in languages that even the learned knew little of. Ritual, ceremonies, the corporal actions of priest and worshippers served only to mask the essentials, for the Kingdom of God was not meat and drink and apparel, but righteousness, peace and joy in the Holy Ghost.[27] These were the spiritual fruits of religion and they demanded a spiritual origin and a spiritual development. Indeed, true religion was the work of the Holy Spirit in the heart leading to man's death to sin in Christ, and his resurrection to righteousness. Preaching was an exposition of what William Haller has called the sacred epic of man's fall and redemption.[28] To Andrewes, preaching had a supporting role as the declaration of the Catholicity of the English Christian Cultus, while to the Puritan, preaching was the primary way in which God spoke to the soul of sinful man in challenge and offer. So preaching was not life to Andrewes or the Arminians, but it was for the Puritan, he had to be a vehicle for the Word and the Spirit. While Andrewes shows an ease with humanism and Renaissance thinking, a wide culture, and a spirituality which saw in the Sacrament a recapitulation of the Gospel in the present,[29] the Puritan Preacher was not at home with humanism which seemed to exalt man above his stature; nor was he terribly interested in Renaissance thinking, since to him, it was mere human knowledge, valuable but not to be intruded into an exposition of the Word. It was the Word that mattered and its

[27] Irvonwy Morgan, *The Godly Preachers of the Elizabethan Church*, pp. 13–20.

[28] William Haller, *The Rise of Puritanism*, p. 19.

[29] John New, *Anglican and Puritan*, p. 67.

spiritual nature had to be spiritually discerned. 'It is the spiritual meaning of the Word let into the heart which converts it unto God.'[30] This is not to say that the Preachers despised or neglected the Sacrament of the Lord's Supper. They believed that to receive the Sacrament was to receive Christ, but, just as Andrewes and his school felt that the mystery of predestination and election were unsuitable for popular enquiry, so the Puritans felt that the manner of Christ's presence in the Sacrament was unfit for enquiry, let alone decision.[31] But they held that at every celebration of the Lord's Supper the Word must be expounded. There was a conjoint significance in the Word and the Sacrament together, which did not adhere to the Sacrament alone. The priestly act needed the prophesying voice effectively to present Christ in the Supper, and prophecy to the Puritan Preacher was the 'opening' of the Word of God.

When the great William Perkins, the theologian of the Elizabethan Puritan Preachers, wrote a treatise on the manner and purpose of preaching, he called it 'The Art of Prophesying' and prophesying was the exposing of the true meaning of the life and death of Jesus Christ as recorded in the Scriptures. The Gospels merely recorded the facts of the life of Christ with special emphasis (more than a third of the Gospel narrative) on the last week of Christ's life, while the 'Acts of the Apostles' recorded the gift of the Holy Spirit and the spread of the Gospel under His guidance by the means of the great Apostle's preaching. The key to the spiritual reality which lay within the life, death and resurrection of Christ was primarily the teaching of St Paul. William Perkins said that if one started the study of the Scriptures with St Paul's 'Epistle to the Romans' and then went on to the 'Gospel of St John,[32] the spiritual meaning of the life of Christ would be laid bare. In particular, the eighth chapter of Romans was the apogee of St Paul's teaching, where the contrast between the life of the spirit and the life of the flesh was asserted, the calling of the elect, and their adoption into Christ expounded, the final victory of those so called to be Saints

[30] Thomas Goodwin, *Works* XI. p. 364.

[31] See an excellent account of the Puritan attitude to the Sacraments in Gordon S. Wakefield's, *Puritan Devotion*, ch. 3.

[32] William Perkins, *Works* II. p. 650.

exposed, 'Whom He foreknew, them he also predestined to be conformed to the image of His Son.' Therefore, no one could lay anything to the charge of God's elect, for it is God alone who justified, and His justification was purely on the faith of the believer in Christ who bore the sins of mankind, and by His death offered Himself a sacrifice to God, thus averting man's just punishment for sin. The calling, justification, sanctification and glorification of the elect was the work of the Spirit, and the purpose of preaching was not only to expound this methodology of Salvation, but much more to expose the working of the Holy Spirit in the human heart. Election was assured to those who were fighting the battle of the spiritual world and it was to identify this battle in the human soul and to enumerate the helps that the Saint received by Grace that was the aim of the Preacher. If a man felt a motion to goodness, that was the work of the Spirit; if he was pricked in his conscience, that was the work of the Spirit; if some action made him feel guilty, that was the work of the Spirit; if he was uplifted by sermon or sacrement, that was the work of the Spirit. 'A Christian furnished with this spiritual life can see Christ and the glory beyond all the things of this life.'[33] The spiritual man can see the vanity of things so admired by others, he can taste things nature does not relish, he has reasons beyond the reasons of the flesh for his attitude, and if he persevered in holy living he would receive his reward in heaven. The marrow of true divinity was the philosophy of St Paul, and it was this divinity which was reproduced by the Holy Spirit in the hearts of the elect. The wind of the Spirit would take a man who set his sails to the wind from the state of destruction and despair to the state of assurance and victory. It was all laid out in Scripture and faithfully interpreted by the great Apostle. 'What do wee', says John Preston to the lawyers of Lincoln's Inn, 'when we dresse up a sermon never so well? It is but the rigging of the sails, and what will all this do without wind? Is not the Spirit the wind? What are organs without breath? There is no musicke made; and what is all our preaching when the Spirit is absent? That is all in all, indeed, it is the sword of the Spirit, but what is it without the almighty hand of God? It is said of one who hearing that 'Scanderbeg's Sword' had done such and

[33] Richard Sibbes, *Saints Cordialls*, p. 280.

such strange work, would needs see it, and sent for the sword, and when he saw the sword he said 'we saw no such matter in it, is this the sword that hath done all this?' Scanderberg sent him word again. 'I have sent the sword but not the arme that handled it.' So, the Word we preach to you is the sword of God—therefore, when you come to heare, pray earnestly that the Arme may go with the sword, that God will make it lively and mighty in operation, to cast down your lusts, to pierce as a two-edged sword, dividing between the bones and the marrow, the joynts and the spirit; that is that you may know yourselves better than you did before; and this use you may make of this, that you are Creatures and no man can make you New Creatures. It is God must do it.'[34] To make you know yourselves better than before, this was the purpose of Puritan preaching, that man should see himself as he really is with his pride stripped from him, his ambitions exposed as selfish egotism, his religion an empty form. When the Puritan preacher had finished with man there was not much left of him to glory in. The Oracle at Delphi advised her enquirers to 'know thyself', but this is the last thing a man will do in reality. If a man is prepared to measure himself by anything at all it is by the 'average', which is tantamount to measuring himself by himself, and this says the Apostle is not wisdom.[35] A man must measure himself by the rule of God. In doing this he sees himself as he truly is—*sub specie aeternitatis.*

[34] John Preston, *The Saint's Qualifications* (The New Creature) (1637), p. 422.

[35] II Corinthians 12:13.

TWO

The Balance of the Sanctuary

WHEN William Perkins told his readers that he stood for the truth, 'that is (as they call it), the Calvanists doctrine' and deplored the way in which students were neglecting the Protestant writers for the fathers and the schoolmen,[1] he expressed what was the main theological ambience of the Puritan Preachers. Perkins, who was Lecturer at Great St Andrewes Church, Cambridge from 1584-1602, rejoiced like all Englishmen at the defeat of Rome and Spain at the Armada, but felt that there was also a need to meet theologically the persistent threat from Rome, and he more than anyone else of his period was able to popularize theology, which made him a best seller with a wide and steadying influence in the churches. William Perkins was a Preacher who did not despise the open-air pulpit erected at Stourbridge Fair in an attempt to win the ear of the masses, and his conversion moved him to act as a Chaplain, preaching to the prisoners in Cambridge Gaol, services which were often attended by 'some of the godly', before he was appointed Preacher at Great St Andrewes.[2] He was what can be called a 'godly preacher', concerned hardly at all with the question of church structures, but with the conversion of souls and their growth in godliness. To him the fundamental question to be asked and answered was 'whether a man was a child of God or not'. This was the ultimate question, for the answer determined a man's eternal future. Perkins and the Godly Preachers who looked to him as at least a learned exponent of their theological views saw the question against a particular background. There was at its base a deep and overwhelming sense of the Majesty

[1] Ian Breward, *William Perkins*, p. 16.
[2] Ibid., p. 8.

of God, coupled with a conviction that man was wilful, proud, arrogant, and selfish, or to put it in the language of the Calvinist thought, a reprobate deserving of God's just punishment, unless he were by God's choice elected to life. But even the elect had no assurance of victory unless they made their election effectual by a life consonant with God's choice. This theology was expounded within the concept of predestination, and in his expositions Perkins gave his solution to this dark New Testament mystery and influenced his contemporaries and successors in the Puritan movement by his sensible and very English practical thought. In his 'Epistle to the Christian Reader', set as an introduction to *A Golden Chain*, or the *Description of Theology* published in 1593, he identifies that there were extant in the Church four several opinions of God's predestination. The first was what he called 'the old and new Palagians' who placed the cause of God's predestination in man in that they held that God did ordain men either to life or death because He foresaw that by their natural free will they would either reject or accept the Grace offered in the Gospel. The second opinion he terms 'Lutheran', which taught that God, seeing that all men were shut up in unbelief, chose some to life of His mere mercy irrespective of their faith and good works, the rest He condemned because He saw that they would eternally reject the Grace offered. The third opinion was of the 'semi-pelagian papists' who ascribed God's predestination partly to mercy and partly to man's foreseen preparation and meritorious works. The fourth opinion taught that God's predestination was His mercy in Christ, in them which are saved and in them that perish in the Fall and Corruption of man. 'Yet, so that the decree of God concerning them both hath not any cause beside His will and pleasure.' Of these four opinions, 'the three former I labour to oppugn as erroneous', says he, 'and to maintain the last as being that which will bear weight in the balance of the Sanctuary'.[3]

The interesting phrase in this introduction to theology is 'the balance of the sanctuary', for although it sounds like a biblical phrase it is not found in the Bible. It is probably original to Perkins and expresses the criteria by which he judged the truth or error of the various opinions on God's predestination. It may

[3] William Perkins, *A Golden Chain* (To the Christian Reader).

be derived from the story of Belshazzar's Feast in the book of Daniel where Daniel interpreted the writing on the wall 'that God had weighed the King in His balance and found him wanting'. John Preston used this phrase on one occasion when he remarked in a sermon that most people judged themselves by the balance of common opinion and not by the balance of the Sanctuary.[4] While Richard Sibbes, in answering in a sermon a rhetorical question, 'Where is Divine Justice now, since God brings evil on His Church, and that by the hand of Idolaters?'[5] tells such questioners to hold their peace, not to take the balance out of God's hand. For the balance of the Sanctuary was the weight one gave in assessing the relation between God's justice and His mercy to men in the decree of predestination. It is significant that of the four opinions current in the Church on the decree summarized by Perkins, the only one which specifically mentions Christ and Christ alone is the one which he supports. The reason for this is that Perkins, and his successors on the Puritan wing of the Church, were preachers first, and theologians second. Their theology subserved their pastoral and evangelical concern for conversion which leads to holiness through the ministration and disciplines of the Church. 'The Elect were predestined to use the means of Grace', says Perkins, 'and by these means a Christian could labour for assurance.'[6] Breward, in his study of Perkins, says that there is more than a hint that Perkins believed assurance to be more important than justification in day to day Christian experience.[7] But the second generation of Puritan Preachers, whose theological ambience we are considering, do not use the word 'assurance' overmuch, and even in Perkins' time there is only a hint of what was to become a key-word in Wesley's preaching. Election to the Puritan Preachers was what assurance was to the Methodist Preachers, for both meant the gift given to the believer, that he might know that he is a redeemed child of God. But both turned on the practical question of man's free will, and on whether in a Christian the will was subordinated to Christ in faith.

[4] John Preston, *Saint's Qualification*, p. 109.
[5] Richard Sibbes, *Saint's Cordialls*, p. 72.
[6] Ian Breward, *William Perkins*, p. 31.
[7] Ibid., p. 85.

The Puritan Preachers defended the scholastic assertion that the elect man could not fall from Grace 'for to hold that an elect Christian may fall away is to pull Christ out of heaven, we are in heaven already in Christ'.[8]

Consequently, if men could be persuaded that they were the elect of God, the Saints destined to triumph in Christ's Kingdom, their struggles gained a dynamic which overthrew all opposition. But, when the Saints had triumphed, and the victory won under Cromwell, this dynamic theology faded into sterile theological argument, which had originated in the great debate with Arminianism. The centre of this debate was the place of man in God's scheme of salvation, namely, could he or could he not choose to reject God's redeeming grace? To the Arminian theologians it seemed plain that the grace of God was offered to all, for Christ died for all according to the Scriptures, and it was within the power of man to refuse that grace, and take the consequences. This stance was anathema to the Calvanists, for, firstly, it insisted that the saving grace of God was offered as well to the reprobate as to the elect, and therefore impugned the decree of God who 'hath mercy on whom He will, and hardens whom He will'; and, secondly, it set man up as the ultimate arbiter of his own eternal destiny and derogated from the power and glory of God. According to the Calvinist when God chose His elect, He brought about their conversion to holiness by an irresistible act of His grace.

From the time of John Calvin's death in 1564 to the time of John Wesley's conversion in 1738, there was almost a complete reversal in the theological and evangelical presentation of Christianity in England. The dominant theological trend in the Church in England in the sixteenth century was Calvinism, whereas the dominant theological trend in the Church in the eighteenth century was 'Arminianism', a term which, following the Laudian divines, sought to identify with the Apostolic Church and that of the Middle Ages. It was in this tradition that Wesley was brought up. Yet the Puritan movement of the sixteenth century was in its own context very similar to the Methodist movement of the eighteenth century. Both movements, for instance, were preaching movements, for the Puritans were

[8] Richard Sibbes, *Saint's Cordialls*, p. 105.

preachers first and foremost and called themselves preachers; similarly the Methodists were preachers first and foremost and called themselves preachers; the aim of both movements was the conversion of souls, and the training of men in holiness. In both movements, spiritual discipline, both as regards loyalty to the means of grace in the Church, and strenuous moral effort for godly living, was a marked characteristic. Faith and good works went together, the one the compliment of the other, and these virtues were exercised in 'classes' bound together by a covenant vow. Both movements created an articulate body of people who took religion seriously within the context of a national Church, and were more like religious orders within a wider Church than separate Churches themselves. But both movements failed to be contained within a national Church and created separate autonomous Churches with marked clerical governmental structures, yet with a strong lay democratic undertone. Both cultivated a simplicity in dress and manners, and had a marked effect on the moral and sociological shape of society. Both the movements were stigmatized with prejorative nicknames, which gradually became acceptable to their adherents and their opponents. But, theologically, the one was the reverse of the other, for the Puritan preachers were convinced Calvinists whilst the majority of Methodist preachers were convinced Arminians.

This theological revolution did not take place without a struggle, and this struggle dominated religion and politics in the Jacobean period. The arena of the confrontation was the Court, and eventually Parliament, and Jacobean Puritanism is significant in that a bold and nearly successful attempt was made to capture the interest of the most powerful of Court personalities, the great Favourite himself, George Villiers, Duke of Buckingham, for the Calvinist cause. It was the patronage of the Duke which placed John Preston in a position of significance at Court, as Chaplain to King Charles, and it was to try to bring the Favourite to declare Calvinism to be the true theological position of the Church of England, that the Conference was held at York House in February 1626[9] between the advocates of Calvinism and Arminianism. John Preston was one of the two

[9] Irvonwy Morgan, *Prince Charles's Puritan Chaplain*, p. 157.

defendants of the Calvinist position at the Conference, the other being Thomas Morton, Bishop of Coventry; while the defenders of Arminianism were John Buckridge, Bishop of Rochester; Richard Montague, later Bishop of Chichester; John Cosin, Canon of Durham; and Francis White, Dean of Carlisle.

The Conference was held in the presence of the Duke of Buckingham and certain noble Lords, and its purpose at least in the minds of the Puritans, led by Lord Saye and the Earl of Warwick, was to accuse Bishop Cosin and Richard Montague and the 'Arminian' party in the Establishment of denying certain specific Articles of the Church of England, and by so doing obtain a resolution from the Favourite to get the Articles of the Synod of Dort recognized as the proper interpretation of the Articles of the Church of England. The Synod of Dort was called by the States General of the Netherlands in 1618, to aid in settling the disputes, theological, personal and political, that had divided the Netherlands for ten or more years. James I had been urging the Dutch to settle the issues by prosecuting the Remonstrants, who came to be called Arminians, and sent four English delegates to the Conference. Among the ecclesiastical delegates, noted divines from all the Reformed churches, there were also eighteen secular commissioners representing Prince Maurice and the States General. Now, whatever Calvin's theological position was on predestination, and it is possible to find in his writings both a 'hard line' and a 'soft line' attitude by emphasizing particular statements of his, by 1618 Calvinism had become so involved in political attitudes, that politics appear more determinative of definitions than theology. H. B. Foster, in his study of the Synod's proceedings,[10] demonstrates quite plainly that the Remonstrants or Liberal Calvinists, later called Arminians, were condemned because Prince Maurice considered them dangerous to the unity of the States General, a unity painfully acquired around the House of Orange in the struggle against Spain. Foster also points out that the belief that they were predestined agents of God, held by both Remonstrants and contra-Remonstrants, was no small factor in their courage

[10] H. B. Foster, *Liberal Calvinism*, Harvard Theological Review, Vol. 16, 1923.

in fighting Spain.[11] It was this stiffening that Prince Maurice still felt was needed, for, though the war with Spain had died down, Spain was still active, and one agent at least of the Papacy in its counter-reformation attack. The Liberal-Calvinists or Arminians under their leader Barneveldte were 'soft' on the Spanish threat, and weak on the concept of predestination, thus eroding the morale of the nation. They were a party in the State rather than a sect in the Church, and it was this political stance which brought about their condemnation. In England, too, Spain cast a tremendous shadow over the scene and during the reign of King James this shadow appeared to acquire substance by the King's conviction that he could make peace with Spain by the marriage of Prince Charles and the Spanish Infanta. Those clergy who supported the King *vis-à-vis* Parliament, and took a very liberal stance about Calvinism came to be called Arminians. The failure of the Puritains to get a 'hard line' Calvinist definition of the Articles according to the Synod of Dort, opened opportunities for the Arminian party to acquire greater influence in the Church and State. So Arminianism came to be associated politically with the autocratic tendencies of the Crown and its Ministers, and theologically with a different mode of presenting the Gospel. Prince Maurice needed a 'hard line' Calvinist definition for political reasons in which Spain loomed large. The Crown in England did not need this dynamic, it had the Channel and the winds of God for its defence against its foes. Consequently, the Puritan assertion, that Arminianism with its apparent pro-Catholic nuances was a danger to the State in its confrontation with Spain, impressed very few people in the Establishment, while the Arminian subservience to the Crown gradually endeared them to King James.

The seventeenth century saw the gradual reversal of the Calvinist mode of presenting the Gospel, from its triumph during the Protectorate, to its retreat after the Restoration, its original flexibility hardening into stultifying theological positions, out of harmony with the expanding Empire and industry in England in the last half of the century. Even such a catholic mind as Baxter found it hard to surrender, and produced a

[11] H. B. Foster, *Liberal Calvinism*, Harvard Theological Review, Vol. 16, p. 16.

middle-way theology which kept the doctrine of election, but repudiated the doctrine of predestination, a halfway house, as it were, to free grace for all. By the time of John Wesley's conversion, Calvinism only lived on in close and somewhat introverted Dissenting Churches, and they too, under the dynamic of the Wesleyan revival, tended to fall into Arminianism despite the power of Whitefield's preaching. Wesley was the true representative of Arminianism in the eighteenth century, and he rejected the Calvinist concept that grace was restricted to the elect alone. Grace was free for all men, through faith, and even though faith was a gift of the Spirit of God, man and man alone was the sole determinative factor for reaching out and accepting the faith. What was started by Arminius in the sixteenth century, in propounding a different mode of presenting the Gospel of Salvation to the Calvinist formula, came to fruition in England in Wesley in the eighteenth century. The whole atmosphere of eighteenth-century England, optimistic, expansive, enterprising, with the prizes of life open to those who could take them was favourable to this change in theology. The felt need was for freedom, freedom of opportunity, freedom to manufacture, freedom to trade, freedom to expand, and life seemed prepared to give all things to those who had the ability to take and make use of them. Consequently, free enterprise, free trade, and free grace belong to the same order of optimism. So the opportunity to receive saving grace was no more restricted or particular than the opportunity to grasp the other good things of life. 'Free grace', says Wesley, 'is all in all.'[12]

In considering this change the Jacobean age was the watershed between the two opposing formulations of the methodology of salvation, and what had once been the dominant theological orientation of the English Establishment was reorientated after the York House Conference giving way to a theological stance which evolved into the Anglican Arminianism of the eighteenth century. John Preston, who somewhat hesitatingly agreed to defend the Calvinist position at the York House Conference, since he really opposed such a confrontation at all, stated his position in a short treatise called *Of the Irresistibleness of Converting Grace.*

[12] John Wesley's *Sermons*, p. 128, sec. 1.

The aim of the treatise was to demonstrate how irresistible grace, which is the logical result of God's decree of election, was compatible with the free will of man. Preston assumes of course that Calvinism was the orthodox faith of the Church, and virtually identifies Arminianism with Pelagianism, which was condemned by Augustine and the Councils of Carthage and Ephesus. He does not go into detail in his identification, it was enough that a similarity was observed. He then quotes Arminiianism to the effect that grace can be resisted by man and that 'an irresistible power and working is not to be attributed unto grace'.[13] His attack on Arminianism begins by comparing the position of the Arminians with that of the Jesuits, in order to demonstrate that Arminianism derogated more from the grace of God than even the Jesuits. Some Jesuits, particularly Saurez, affirmed that sufficient grace was given to all, even to the reprobates, but effectual grace which infallibly converts, was given only to the elect. The Jesuits however placed the efficacy of effectual grace not in a physical determination of the will as the Calvinists did, but in a moral persuasion as the Arminians did. The Jesuits however conceived that this moral persuasion was irresistible in certain cases, by developing the doctrine of *Congruity*, that is a persuasion offered with such circumstances as Place, Person and Time, as to which God (who from everlasting knows the inclinations of the will) foresees that the will shall infallibly yield. So the Jesuits attributed conversion wholly to the good pleasure of God and that congruous or suitable calling was peculiar to the elect. The Arminians on the other hand denied the infallible calling of the elect; the Holy Spirit might be resisted even when he works upon a man with the intent of conversion. Consequently, says Preston, the Arminian divines were more dangerous to the true doctrines of conversion than were the Jesuits. The ultimate enemy might be the Papists, but they had been decisively defeated in England by the destruction of the Spanish Armada in the previous reign and were therefore more remote than the Arminians who were immediately active and indeed occupied some of the best bishoprics and deaneries in the English Church.

[13] John Preston, *Of the Irresistibleness of Converting Grace* (Tracts and Sermons, 1616–54), p. 2.

The focal point of this confrontation of ideas was in the nature of the freedom of the will and how it had been affected by the Fall.[14] To the Arminians, free will was 'like the power of moving, in one who is bound in fetters, or the faculty of seeing, in one who is shut up in a dark place'. 'Whereas we hold', says Preston, 'that the faculty of the will, as it respects a truly spiritual good is wholly extinct, as the power of life in a dead man, of motion in a slaine man, of sight in those whose eyes are put out.'[15] It is only a small step intellectually from the Arminian position to the philosophy of Rousseau and the enlightenment of the next century, 'that man is *born* free, but is everywhere in chains', one of the chains being religion!

The Arminian view of the gift of grace is therefore irrelevant to the problem of salvation. For the problem of salvation is not how God may assist a man who has already chosen the good, but how a corrupt man may even choose the good. 'To will', says Preston, quoting Augustine, 'is of ourselves, but to will well, both partly and wholly is of grace.'[16] Consequently, the will must, in fact, be made good, before it can perform any spiritual work, and this is not performed by persuading grace, but by healing and regenerating grace. The habitual aversion of the will from God, and its perversion to sensual and carnal things, must be changed by an infusion of habitual grace imprinted on the will. No man sees, he says, unless he first have eyes, nor hears unless he has ears, so in spiritual things, no man sees or hears unless God first gave him eyes to see and ears to hear. So, a man must be given a new heart, that is a new will to turn and love God. This regenerating grace, however, does not destroy the will but controls it. His view owes quite a lot to the Schoolmen, and he quotes Aquinas with approval. He holds the scholastic view that God is the cause of the whole Being, but that sin is not a being but a defect of what should be in a faculty or act, and claims that the more ancient Schoolmen do not support Saurez and the Jesuits in their view of grace. He indicates that there are some views of irresistible grace which

[14] John Preston, *The Irresistibleness of Converting Grace* (Tracts and Sermons, 1616–54), p. 13.

[15] Ibid., p. 7.

[16] Ibid., p. 4.

are not consonant with the freedom of the will, but he held that though the will does act in conversion it does so only when the grace of faith is planted in the heart, and, in a secondary manner, subordinate to the infinite power of God who wills the conversion of those whom He chooses.

The will, he argues, cannot resist an enlightened understanding which has been convinced by reason, for reason only is the root and foundation of liberty or freedom. It follows then, that only acts of the will which reason has influenced are truly free. Indeed, the will is only free when it flows from a reasonable persuasion. Conversion is therefore a supernatural act of grace and provided from the same power whereby Christ was raised from the dead. Consequently, a man does not 'will or run that God might have mercy on him, and regenerate him by the quickening grace of the Spirit, but because God first hath mercy, therefore he willeth and runneth in the way of righteousness'.[17] A wheel, he says, does not run well that it may be round, but because it is round it runs well, so a man is not holy that he may be converted, for this is impossible to the fallen and corrupt nature of man, he who is chosen is converted irresistibly by God's grace in order that he may become holy. And that any man by an act of the will can resist God's absolute and peremptory Decree must not be imagined.[18]

Arminianism was however a plausible explanation of the fact that all men did not act as believing Christians. Some lived righteous lives and some did not and both seemed to choose themselves the kind of lives they would live. It was a far more simplistic explanation than the Calvinist one and matched theologically as it were the expanding humanism of Renaissance thinking. On the other hand Calvinism offered a different explanation of the fact that some men were righteous and some were not. It was not their choice but that of the inscrutable will of God whereby He chose some to life and passed others by.

Yet, Calvinism had its problems, particularly to the Preacher. It was one thing to work out a logical theory to explain the sin and waywardness of man with respect to the sovereign grace and power of God, but, if man's eternal destiny was God's decision,

[17] *The Irresistibleness of Converting Grace* (Tracts and Sermons), p. 14.
[18] Ibid., p. 17.

and God's alone, why should a man bother to be holy? If God destined a man to be holy He would make him so. This was no Gospel for the evangelical preacher who knew that men had to be exhorted to righteousness, and warned of the damnable consequences of their sins. Calvinism, therefore, tended psychologically, at least, to undermine the urgency of a moral imperative, and might indeed result in antinomianism.

The Preachers, therefore, had to produce some acceptable way of presenting the balance of the sanctuary so as to emphasize the necessity of a real moral effort in the attainment of salvation. They solved this, practically at least, in assuming that no man was elected unless he was a candidate! As far as they were concerned in their preaching a man had to demonstrate by his life that he was truly a candidate for heaven. They did not put it as crudely as this, but they used various theological devices to attain the same ends. William Perkins, systematized in his *Treatise of Vocations,* one such limitation. The elect, he says, have a general calling to the Christian life, but they, with every man, are placed by God in particular callings which demand the exercise of moral virtues, such as honesty, compassion, goodness and so on. Indeed, he says, the general calling of Christianity without the practice for some particular calling is 'nothing else but the form of Godliness without the power thereof'.[19] The right way to reformation of life for any man is to ask himself what is his particular calling and then to practise the duties of this Christian life in that calling. This very practice differentiated men into good men and bad men. 'So', says he, 'if thou wouldst have signs and tokens of thy election and salvation, thou must fetch them from the constant practice of these two callings jointly together.'[20] Another way of saying the same thing is illustrated in a phrase sometimes used, that the elect must make their calling or election 'effectual'. It is too simple to say that this means that any man who lived a good Christian life was therefore one of the elect of God, but it seemed to convey something of that conclusion.

But a flexible way in which the exclusion rigorism of second generation Calvinist theology was modified by the Preachers

[19] William Perkins, *Works*, p. 1, 751A.
[20] Ibid., p. 1, 757.

was by the development of what may be called Covenant Theology. In essence, a covenant is an agreement between two or more persons to behave to each other in a particular way. John Preston in his sermons on the New Covenant sometimes uses the terms 'contract' or 'league' as synonyms. Covenant theology was not something invented by the Puritan Preachers, they merely used the concept of a covenant between God and man in a new way, for a covenant produced an artificial brotherhood where the natural brotherhood of parish or nation did not provide an adequate incentive for a course of action. Richard Rogers, one of the earliest of Puritan Preachers, never mentions covenant theology in his *Seven Treatises*, but in the fifth treatise he mentions a covenant made by about twenty godly brethren of his parish to live godly and disciplined lives. Such a covenant became a mark of the gathered Church, separating the covenant group from the natural brotherhood of a parish. But a further development of the covenant idea was expressed in the theological thinking of men like William Ames, John Preston and Richard Sibbes, and through their sermons communicated to many of the New England Divines. This extended the idea of a covenant from an agreement between a group of people, to the concept of an agreement between God and man, of which there were many examples in the Old Testament, for God made covenants with all the Patriarchs and particularly with Abraham, the Father of the Faithful, which covenant was ratified by the Sacrifice of Christ in the New Israel of the Church.

John Preston was one of the greatest exponents of Covenant Theology, and his teaching on this aspect of Christian life and thinking is to be found in the collection of sermons published under the title of *The New Covenant*. In the tenth sermon he explains what is meant by the covenant between God and man. There is, he says, a double covenant, a covenant of works and a covenant of grace. The covenant of works applies to all men, and it runs: 'Do this, and thou shalt live, and I will be thy God.'[21] This is really another way of expressing the conviction that all men are under the law, and if they obey the law they shall live and God will be their God. This is the covenant made with Adam and Moses, and is expressed in the moral law. The

[21] *The New Covenant*, p. 71.

Covenant of Grace, however, was in these terms: 'Thou shalt believe, thou shalt take my Sonne for thy Lord and thy Saviour, and thou shalt likewise receive the gift of righteousness which was wrought by Him for an absolution of their sinnes, for a reconciliation with me, and whereupon thou shalt grow up into love and obedience toward me, then I will be thy God and thou shalt be my people.[22] The Covenant of Grace begins not with obedience to the law, but with belief in Christ as Lord and Saviour. The gift of righteousness which accompanies conversion is the gift of a working faith, a faith which has life and power in it. But it is a faith that works by love, and nothing that a man does has any spiritual value at all, even preaching the Gospel, or giving a cup of water to a dying man, unless it is done for the love of Christ and an exceeding desire to please Him. In the covenant are the promises of God, the promise of salvation, the promise of sanctification. 'If a man believes God now', says Preston, 'it makes him a partaker of the Covenant. You will say, this is very strange, how can it be that so small a condition as this, that to believe, should make a man a partaker of the Covenant; that upon which all the promises hang initially, is nothing but believing!'[23] The Covenant is not a Commandment, do this and that, the Covenant is a promise: 'I will give thee, etc.,' and it is faith that answers a promise, for a promise is to be believed. Preston then faces the question, 'May a man believe this promise, and yet walk according to the lusts of his own ignorance and be made a partaker of the Covenant?' 'Let him', he says, 'if he can believe truly and do this, but it is impossible.'[24] It is this challenge to the believer, which inserts as it were a moral imperative into the rigour of Calvinist theology. A Believer must fight Satan relying on the promises of God. The Covenant made with God was not a once only occasion. It could be and indeed had to be renewed as part of the conditional effort of man to keep his part of the agreement. These times of renewal are often recorded in Puritan diaries, as times of repentance for past failures and a determination to persevere in the godly life. These opportunities for the renewal of the

[22] *The New Covenant*, p. 145.
[23] Ibid., p. 114.
[24] Ibid., p. 115.

covenant vow are especially true of the Sacrament of the Lord's Supper. 'You have cause to make use of this time, when you receive the Sacrament. For what do you? You come to renew your Covenant with God.'[25] For the Covenant of Grace under which the believer lives was ratified by the greatest sacrifice of all, the shedding of the blood of the Son of God Himself. Yet, it was not enough merely to make a vow of repentance all over again on these occasions, they were also occasions when God could be challenged to keep his promise of aid in the Spiritual warfare.[26] Preston uses an extraordinary metaphor in his twelfth sermon to emphasize this, for the believer is entitled to 'opresse' the promises, 'as a rich man oppresseth a poor man and gets out of him all that he is worth, he leaves him worth nothing, he plays the extortioner with him; after that manner deal thou with the promises, for they are rich, there is a price in them, and be thou as an extortioner to them, take them out whatsoever thou needest, or wring it out of the promises, as it were.'[27] But men were not entitled to challenge God in this way, as they were men and unregenerate, for in this state they lived under the law, and obeyed if they could, in fear of the wrath of God. Believers, however, were in a different state, because they had been baptized with the Holy Spirit, which made them Prophets, Priests, and Kings, and favourites of the Court of Heaven.[28]

The place of the covenant in the economy of Grace then provided a sphere for the growth of a doctrine of assurance, for if a man was predestined for heavenly glory he was predestined to use the means of Grace and this included the performance of good works and union with Christ. In fact, a doctrine of union with Christ which leads to co-operation with God and a renewal of the defective nature of man in repentance and conversion seemed to some to introduce a further conditional note in the doctrine of election and reprobation. It seemed to emphasize that the soul must be prepared to receive Christ, and the more a man prepared then the more help he found in the Grace of God. But this 'preparation' did not mean that by acquiring good habits

[25] Ibid., p. 194.
[26] Ibid., p. 136.
[27] Ibid., p. 231.
[28] Ibid., p. 212.

a man was preparing by his own natural inclinations to receive the Grace of God. This was the error of the Pelagians 'who ascribe the beginnings, preparations, and abilities, of our accepting Grace for ourselves, and of our own free-will, although the compliment be of God'.[29] In acquired habits, says Preston, the act goes before the habits and prepares for it. But in infused habits it is as with the natural powers of the soul, which has the faculty of seeing before it sees, and of hearing before it hears. So men must have the infused habits of Grace before they exercise the operations of it, 'so the heart doth not first see the action whereby it may be set in a good frame but it is first fashioned, and made a new creature by Grace, and then it doth perform actions'.[30] This refashioning of the heart is only possible when men are satisfied with Christ 'and goe to Christ as Bees to a Meddow full of flowers, and as Merchants to the Indies that are full of wines and spices, that you may feel, experimentally, yourselves return from him full-fraught with the treasures of truth and Grace'.[31] For the union between the believer and Christ is a perfect union 'we are in Him, as the branches are in the vine'. Nothing puts so high a degree of excellence in the believer than this, for this union is closer than that of man and wife. It is closer than the union of grain mixed with grain, and water with water. It is to possess the life of Christ Himself, in comparison with which all other things are vain and full of deceit.[32] The operative words are 'to feel experimentally' that union with Christ which is the dynamic of Christian action and witness and this is merely another way of stating what became in the next century the doctrine of assurance as preached by the new Puritans, John Wesley and his helpers.

In the balance of the sanctuary as between the justice and mercy of God, redeeming Grace was only received by God's 'secret ones'. For God hid the excellency of Christ from the world 'under a base outside', so that only the chosen of God could find it, and others (truly blinded) only stumbled at it. Such

[29] John Preston, *The Fullness of Christ for Us* (1640), p. 14.
[30] Ibid., p. 15.
[31] Ibid., p. 7.
[32] John Preston, *An Elegant and Lively Description of Life and Death*, pp. 53–6.

preparations as were needed were only 'to trample on the glory of the world' for His sake, to turn away from the vanities of fleshly existence, and to pitch all affections and thoughts on him',[33] to repent at the thought of how one should spend eternity. It behoved men to make sure of their election yet not in idleness because all Grace is received, for the believer must work out his salvation in fear and trembling in thankfulness to God for His mercy, in humility towards men 'for what have we that we have not received', and lastly, 'be begging Grace at God's hand by prayer'.[34] For in obtaining anything merely given and received, that is the proper means. As prayer is said to be the *banquet of Grace*, so it is then that *a man of much prayer is a man of much Grace.*[35]

In the balance of the Sanctuary the scales were therefore weighted in favour of Christ, God's own elect one and those whom He had chosen. To know whether one had been weighed in the balance of God's justice and mercy and found wanting, or whether one had been chosen to be a child of God, demanded a continuous appeal to God for Grace in prayer. It was by prayer that the believer renewed his repentance and lived by Grace within the terms of the Covenant and by experience became conscious of God's mercy to him. It was by prayer that he set his heart straight with God day by day, and 'This', says Preston, 'is the very life of religion.'[36]

[33] John Preston, *The Fullness of Christ for Us*, pp. 8 and 9.
[34] Ibid., p. 22.
[35] Ibid., p. 22.
[36] Ibid., p. 22.

THREE

The Market Day of the Soul

PROFESSOR Gordon Rupp points out in *Patterns of Reformation* that Sabbatarianism is more a characteristic of Luther's contemporary Andreas Carlstadt than it is of either Luther or Calvin, and has a greater affinity with Puritanism than with Reformation teaching and practice.[1] It may even be said that Sabbatarianism was more a Catholic than a Protestant emphasis. 'So far is Sabbatarianism from being a later English and Puritan invention that it is part of a very early and widespread Christian tradition, Catholic in a far truer sense than many other observances that claim that title.'[2] It was always possible to suffer in the Middle Ages for breaking the Sabbath, for Canon Law, though it was more often observed in the breach perhaps, insisted that Sabbath should be spent exclusively on nothing save God, for it was the Lord's Day. The only works allowed on the Sabbath were works of charity, for the day must be spent on purely pious and intellectual exercises.

Something of Carlstadt's emphasis on the Sabbath had been communicated to the English Reformers through that doyen of the Continental Reformers, Martin Bucer, who found a refuge in Cambridge as Regius Professor of Divinity, when Strasbourg, where he had taught for twenty years, fell to the armies of the Emperor. He only lectured in Cambridge for some fifteen months however before he died, but during that time he published his pattern of reformation for England under the title *De Regno Christi* (1550) which was the substance of his lectures at the University. As he told Calvin, 'I am permitted to set forth the Kingdom of Christ with the most entire freedom in my lectures,

[1] Gordon Rupp, *Patterns of Reformation* (1968), pp. 123–30.
[2] G. C. Coulton, *Mediaeval Panorama* (1949), p. 181.

disputations, and Latin sermons.'[3] Not that Bucer pleased the extreme English reformers of his time, he was too moderate in such issues as the vestment controversy and approved, though guardedly, of the Book of Common Prayer. But, there were certain elements in his teaching which did appeal to them, namely, his emphasis on Church discipline, and, more particularly perhaps, his insistence on Sabbath observance, which he wished to see enforced by Royal Command. In this he anticipated the teaching and practice of the Puritan Preachers who one and all pressed for the sanctification of the Sabbath both by precept, and by agitation, through their friends in Parliament. Sabbatarianism is one of the great frames of the Puritan movement, and no appreciation of Puritanism is possible without some understanding of the Puritan love for and respect for the Sabbath day.

In the sense of freedom which was generated by the revolt from Rome, many Reformers claimed a freedom from religious observances such as holy-days, and the ceremonial attached to them. In these freedoms was often included freedom from Sabbath observances. 'Man is Lord of the Sabbath' was their cry, and the defender of Sabbatarianism at the dawn of the English Reformation was not William Tyndale, the Protestant, but rather Sir Thomas More, the Catholic.[4] To the Reformers all these observances were the 'meat, drink, new moons and Sabbaths' that the Apostle Paul had condemned. They were merely the shadows of things to come, the fulfilment was Christ, and in His freedom all these observances were abrogated. Calvin had discussed the question of the observance of the Sabbath in *The Institutes of the Christian Religion*, when commenting on the Commandment, 'Remember the Sabbath Day to keep it Holy', and recognized that Sabbath observance was part of the ceremonial Law of Israel. Since the Law had been fulfilled in Christ, even the Jewish Sabbath was, with other Jewish ceremonies abolished, for, as St Paul taught, it was superstitious to make one day differ from another in spiritual significance. This was one aspect of the spiritual freedom brought to the believer in Christ. However, Calvin was a churchman and knew that it

[3] Quoted in H. C. Porter, *Reformation and Reaction in Tudor Cambridge*, p. 53.

[4] Gordon S. Wakefield, *Puritan Devotion*, p. 59.

was impossible to persuade people to that holiness, without which no man could see the Lord, except by a discipline of the spiritual life. This discipline demanded an arrangement whereby the people assembled on stated days for the hearing of the Word, the breaking of the mystical bread, and public prayer,[5] and it was within the competence of the Church, said Calvin, to order these stated days. He agreed that it would be a great privilege to hold daily meetings for these purposes, as some argued, and so avoid the distinction of days, but the weakness of the flesh would not allow it, and the charity of the Church would not exact more than was reasonable from this weakness. It was however appropriate for the Christian to follow God's example, who did all His work in the Creation of the World in six days and rested on the seventh. Calvin observes, in addition, that as our Lord was raised from the dead on the first day of the week, the Church was competent to set this day aside as its Sabbath to retain decency, order and peace in the Church, that men might have opportunity to observe the prior demand made on them by God, to mortify the flesh in meditation on the Kingdom of God, and to do so by using the means God has appointed for this end.

Calvin's subtle handling of Scripture to maintain the traditional Sabbath without relying on Jewish precedents or giving way to extremist libertarians, was too subtle for English Puritans. They, in general, tended to rely on Old Testament precedent, particularly the fact that even before the Fall a Sabbath rest was necessary for Adam to maintain even him in his innocency. But the arguments used by John Dod, Lewis Bayley, or Richard Greenham, or even Nicholas Bownd, whose *True Doctrine of the Sabbath*—first published in 1595—had an immense vogue in England and the Continent was not the fundamental reason for the Puritan devotion to the Sabbath. It was something deeper and more human, something elemental in the heart of religion, and its need to make foci, around which sentiment, devotion and piety might gather.

Puritan worship in its ideal form demanded an austere, intellectual, and spiritual approach. Its great adversary was cere-

[5] John Calvin, *The Institutes of the Christian Religion*, I, p. 341.

monial religion, best exemplified by Catholicism, and in its attenuated form, by the worship of the Church of England. In the overthrow of the Roman Catholic presentation of the Christian faith in England, a multitude of small foci or religious emotion and practice were destroyed. No longer did the English expression of religion centre around genuflections or incantatory prayers. There was now no holy water, no votive candles, no incense, no sacred images, no blazing altars, no ritual movements, no solemn distant chants, no rustling priests, no prostrate nuns, no magnificent processions, no obit days, no magic windows, no wayside shrines, no gentle Virgin, no baby Jesus, no suffering Christ, on which to gaze and weep; no liquifying blood, no miraculous cures, no passionate pilgrimages. In fact, a whole world of religious acts around which piety could be cultivated was destroyed and the Church was left with the bare bones of worship in Word, Sacraments and holy discipline. Even prayer was not to be systematized but left to the free influence of the Spirit and the inspiration of the moment. The Church of England, in which the Puritan Preachers served, had compromised with the Reformation, or, so they thought, for she still retained some of the 'dregs of Rome' in hierarchy of vestments, and a liturgy. She, too, needed to complete the Reformation and a great deal of discussion in Elizabethan and Jacobean Puritan Conferences is taken up with the question of how far a man could submit to these observances without compromising spiritual religion.[6] For the Puritan had been taught by John Foxe that the Christian was not the 'ceremonial man after the Church of Rome, but the spiritual man with his faith and other fruits of piety following the same'.[7] But no religion can be so spiritual that it has no need of time and place, and the time for the Puritan Preacher was primarily the Sabbath day and the place the Church with its minimum of ceremonial objects, the great pulpit Bible from the interpretation of which was offered the audible Gospel, and the bread and the wine of the Sacrament of Christ's

[6] Irvonwy Morgan, *The Godly Preachers of the Elizabethan Church*, pp. 152–74.

[7] John Foxe, *The Acts and Monuments of the Christian Martyrs*, p. xxxii.

death and passion which was the 'visible Gospel'.[8] These, with the attendant fast days and conferences, were the foci of religious devotion and spiritual piety from which sprang the dynamic of the Puritan Movement.

The Sabbath had a greater significance for Puritans as a focus for piety and devotion than for any other religious groups and certainly for the Established Church—not only because the setting aside of a day for worship was part of a long Christian tradition which they could accept, nor because of the Biblical precedents of the Old and New Testaments, but because the Sabbath gave a context in which the purposes of Puritanism could be exploited. This purpose was to bring men to conversion and train them in holiness. The Sabbath was not the only time when this could be done, for the 'Prophesyings', 'Fasts', and 'Conferences', were also such occasions. These however were subsidiary to the Sabbath exercises and never took their place. Puritan piety was in some respects the antithesis of the idea that religion was the 'flight of the alone to the alone'; to them, as to John Wesley, a solitary Christian was a contradiction in terms,[9] Even the private duties of religion, such as self-examination, finding out one's sinful ways, meditation on the Word, prayer, visiting the sick and poor, were undertaken to prepare the heart to profit by the public exercise of religion on the Sabbath.[10]

Consequently, it is a misunderstanding of Puritanism to over emphasize its individualism. S. R. Gardiner makes this mistake, for instance, in discussing the Puritan attitude to Sabbath observance. He says of the Puritan 'however desirable it might be to go to church upon the Sabbath, the Puritan could do all that was necessary for the observance of the day without crossing his own threshold. The main thing lay in his own emotional thoughts, and in his careful abstinence from merely secular labours and pleasures'.[11] The fact is that to the Puritan the

[8] John Preston, *The Saint's Qualification* (1637), p. 485.

[9] John Preston, *The Golden Sceptre* (1639) (The Church's Carriage), p. 141.

[10] John Dod, *The Ten Commandments* (1635), p. 133.

[11] S. R. Gardiner, *Prince Charles and the Spanish Marriage* (1869), Vol. 1, p. 198.

Sabbath was the 'Lord's Day', and the church was 'God's House', and it was in 'God's House, that the Word was publicly preached and the Sacraments rightly administered'.[12]

It is not therefore without significance that one of the analogies used by the Puritans to describe the Sabbath Day is that it was the 'Market Day of the Soul'. The phrase is used by both John Dod and Richard Greenham, two of the most influential of Elizabethan and Jacobean Puritan Preachers, and Greenham emphasizes this approach to the Sabbath by calling it, in addition, 'the Faire-Day Of The Soule'.[13] The phrase the 'Market Day of the Soul' has no particular significance today, simply because Markets and Fairs have lost their importance, particularly their social importance. Buying and selling, which was the basic reason for Market Days is done differently today; consequently, the occasions for social intercourse which such a medium of exchange provided have declined. If we can think back into the seventeenth century we can see that Market days were the great regular social occasions for the community. Every week in town and country, people gathered together at Market. Families met each other, letters were collected from far off friends, and sent to friends by carriers; politics were discussed; the gentry and county families mixed with farmers and artisans; merchants and montebanks displayed their wares; news was gathered of doings at Court and of foreign states; labourers, maids and apprentices had a day off; the hard grind of daily work was relaxed. It was a holiday for all, though for the farmer, the merchant, the master who needed men, and the labourer who needed to be hired, the peddlar with his pack, and a host of others, it was an opportunity to do business, to buy what one needed, and to sell what one could spare. As Market Day was a day set aside by authority for trafficking in earthly things, so Sunday was a day set aside by God for trafficking in heavenly things; it was the Lord's Day. It was not a day for a man merely to disappear into his closet for meditation on the Word and its meaning for the soul, but that having been done, it was a day when he had spiritual conference with his neighbour in the public exercise of religion. It was a day when he could hear once again good news

[12] John Dod, *The Ten Commandments* (1635), p. 133.
[13] Richard Greenham, *Works*, p. 159.

from a far country, the good news of sins forgiven and grace offered in Christ the Lord of the Day; a day when the company of the faithful, the elect of God, the people of the Covenant could rejoice in the saving mercy of God and receive the Spirit of God.

As a man going to Market had to prepare for it by thinking of what he wanted for his needs, and what he could discard by way of sale; by providing sufficient money to buy what he wanted when the opportunity occurred; by clearing up his work so that the day might be completely free, so the Godly man would prepare for the Market Day of his Soul. The work of the week had to be done to leave the Sabbath free, so that the time that God demanded of him for the care of his soul was not frittered away by earthly cares. The godly discipline of his own household, by which some part of each day was given to self-examination, to meditation on the Word of God, and to prayer, exposed his defects and defeats in the spiritual life which could be rectified in the public exposition of the Word, and mutual Conference and discussion with friends on the Sabbath Day. On the Sabbath Day the means of Grace were exposed in promise and precept for his salvation. It was a day consecrated to God, and as John Dod said, 'There is as much difference between the Sabbath Day and other days, as between the consecrated bread we receive at the Lord's Table, and the common bread we receive at our own table.'[14]

Whether or not a man received a blessing in Sabbath worship depended on how he approached it. John Dod summarized this approach under these precepts. First of all a man must make it 'a delight to keep the Lord's Day and a joy to do the works of the Sabbath'. He must long for it before it comes, and be glad when it does come, and come hungry for the bread of life to the House of God. Secondly, he must do all the duties of the Sabbath; meditation on God's Word, hearing, reading, praying, singing Psalms, conference and works of mercy, and 'of everything, something'. The fewer of these works he performs the fewer blessings he will have. 'He that does God's service by halves shall . . . find comfort and benefit of these by halves.' Thirdly, he must do all the duties with delight, he must keep the whole day, the whole twenty-four hours for God, because 'He who com-

[14] John Dod, *The Ten Commandments*, p. 124.

mands us to keep the Sabbath in the church, bids us keep it in the house also'.[15] In other words, the Sabbath is the main focus in time and the House of God with its means of Grace, the main focus in space around which piety and devotion must centre for the godly.

John Dod was a personal friend of John Preston and also the patriarch of the Puritan party from whom Preston, as its leader, received much counsel and advice. Preston himself never preached any sermon exclusively on Sabbath observance, but in enumerating the duties of the godly life, keeping the Sabbath was well to the fore. He did expand on the duty of keeping the Sabbath on one occasion when perhaps he thought it would do most good, not when he was preaching at Court, but on the one occasion when he preached before Parliament in July 1625, the Parliament which did tighten up Sunday observance by ruling that men could not leave their parishes on Sundays for recreational purposes. The Puritans all objected to secular recreation, hawking, gambling, hunting and so on, on the Sabbath, but the law allowed such things. King James himself had published his *Book of Sports* in support of the law, partly in answer to Nicholas Bownd's book, in which such recreations on Sunday were condemned. The fact that Preston never pressed Sabbath observance in his sermons at Court may be due to his tactful approach to the King! On the other hand, there was pressure in Parliament for a stricter control of the Sabbath from the Puritan group of which Lord Saye, a personal friend of John Preston, was in some measure the leader. Preston used this opportunity to emphasize the sanctification of the Sabbath in what he called a 'digression'.[16] His argument is based on a text in Isaiah 57:30, that God claimed the Sabbath day as 'My Holy Day'. He differed from Calvin who believed it was in the competence of the Church to decide on the day, holding that God did not leave it merely to the Church to decide. It was God's Day, and to use it for any ends other than the service of God was to rob Him of His time. He also emphasized the antiquity of the practice, quoting both Justin Martyr and Tertullian; and finally asserts that the text 'The Sabbath was made for man's means that God had

[15] Ibid., pp. 164–5.

[16] John Preston, *The Saint's Qualification* (1637), p. 237.

instituted the day for man's sake lest he should 'forget God and become a stranger to Him'.[17] John Preston however was well aware of the accusation made against the Puritans that sanctifying the Sabbath was a return to legalist Judaism and therefore it was merely a cover for hypocrisy. 'Yee may call sanctifying the Sabbath, Judaism, yee may call strictness of life Hypocrisie and Preciseness; Zeale, indiscretion, but what say your consciences of them? If that which we doe be but hypocrisie, why doe you not it in reality?'[18] Sanctifying the Sabbath was part of the Puritan challenge to the Church to take seriously the religion they professed. His appeal in this as in other things was to the consciences and not to the 'wits and humours of men'.

This insistence on Sabbath observance by the Puritan Preachers was fundamentally derived from the fact that it was one of the few avenues open to them to impress religion on the minds of the people.

To make the matter of keeping the Sabbath a matter of conscience was something that could only be first developed in the home, for religion to the Puritan was family religion, and Sunday worship was family worship. The ideal that was set before men in the preaching of the Word was the ideal of holiness, without which no man could see the Lord. It was to produce Saints, men strong in the ways of godly living, confirmed in the union with Christ 'doing earthly things with a heavenly mind'. It was the same aim as the monk while at the same time remaining engaged in the active life of the world.[19] This ideal demanded a regular disciplined life of prayer and service, for good works were as necessary as prayer, and, indeed, only truly spring from a life of prayer. It also demanded a close community, which the monk found in the cloister, where virtue could be continually executed. The family was the right place for this daily walking in grace, and it is no surprise to learn that 'God's graces may as well be exercised in the family as in the cloyster'.[20] The family was a 'little church' presided over by the father who was priest or pastor to his flock. The flock included, of course, not only the

[17] John Preston, *The Saint's Qualification* (1637), p. 238.
[18] John Preston, *The Doctrine of Self-Denial* (1632), p. 65.
[19] L. L. Schucking, *The Puritan Family* (1969), p. 58.
[20] William Perkins, *Works* I, p. 586.

children, but servants, apprentices, and any workmen who lived with the family. Every day there were family prayers and bible-study, and opportunity for psalm-singing. There were times set aside for catechizing the children, and for discussing the sermons heard during the week. Every day the church came into the family as it were, and confirmed their efforts. Here attempt was made, to use the words of Schucking, to create cell by cell, the new political entity, the great religious 'beehive';[21] family cells of disciplined religious living, circulating around the church and the Sabbath as the two great foci of piety and devotion.

When Ben Jonson gave the name of Zeal-of-the-Land Busy to the comic character of a Puritan in his play *Bartholomew Fair* he not only put his finger on two characteristics of the Puritan, zeal and busyness, but also added to the carricature the words 'A Banbury Man'. Banbury was one of the centres of Puritanism towards the end of the Elizabethan era. It was the market town of the Saye and Sele family who lived at Boughton Castle nearby, and there was no more dedicated Puritan than Lord Saye. William Teelinck, the Father of Dutch pietism, stayed for nine months in Banbury in 1604, and described in the preface of his *Huysboeck* the ethos of the town and the family with whom he stayed. Many families were organized in the manner described above with family prayers twice a day, bible-reading before breakfast, and at midday before lunch. Weekday sermons were reverently attended, and all this was orientated to the central point of Sunday worship. On the Sabbath the town was quiet and free from noise, except that the singing of psalms could be heard from some of the houses. The two sermons were well attended and often taken down in shorthand by experts. These sermons invariably formed the subject for discussion at meals and also in the evenings in the presence of children and servants who were catechized as to what they remembered. Sunday evenings, too, gave an opportunity for free discussion of any grudge that any member of the household held against another. Aid for the poor, visiting the sick and the oppressed, were regular duties conscientiously performed.[22] Teelinck also says that unbelievers in the town were compelled to keep quiet out of consideration

[21] L. L. Schucking, *The Puritan Family*, p. 57.
[22] Ibid., pp. 57 and 58.

for the rest. This kind of Sabbath observance and disciplined family piety grew throughout the century, survived the Restoration of Charles II, was re-inforced by the Methodist Revival in the eighteenth century, and formed the characteristic expression of Protestant piety, in the nineteenth century. Such a devotion to the Sabbath, to the Word, and to the religious family discipline indeed lasted to within living memory. With its decline has come the decline of family fellowship and parental discipline, and the rise of all those elements in secular life such as the limiting of families by contraception and abortion which were heinous sins to the Puritan.[23] For the Puritan idea of the family was in line with the great Christian tradition that children, the home, and the Christian home in particular, were gifts of God. When the service of God was rightly performed, the home became a kind of Paradise on earth,[24] which mirrored in miniature the Paradise in Heaven to which men were pointed by public testimony in Word and Sacrament, Sabbath by Sabbath.

In whatever area Puritanism increased its hold on the clergy and people, pressure was exercised by them to separate the Sabbath day as a special day for the worship of God only. The Puritan Conference which met at Dedham in Essex between the years 1582–9 succeeded in persuading the clothiers and dyers of the area not to work on Sunday, but to encourage their workmen to go to church! Thomas Gataker, the Puritan son of the Earl of Leicester's domestic chaplain, was the Preacher at Lincoln's Inn from 1601–13, and during this period he persuaded the Lawyers of the Inn not to work on Sundays, as an example to the lower orders. In the 1614 Parliament, two of the Puritan Lords, Lord Saye and the Earl of Warwick, presented a bill to Parliament for the better observance of the Sabbath. Yet despite this sort of pressure the Puritans succeeded in getting the Sabbath observed as they thought it ought to be observed only among the people who supported the Preachers. Richard Baxter, for instance, who became Lecturer at Kidderminster in the 1620s tells us that when he went to Kidderminster only about one family in each street went to church, but he left a town of

[23] Richard Sibbes, *Saint's Cordialls*, p. 142, and Schucking, *The Puritan Family*, p. 67.

[24] William Perkins, *Works* III, p. 691.

about 1,600 inhabitants who were for the most part practising Christians, and that there were some streets where every family attended church. Within a year or two of his going to Kidderminster the capacious church had five extra galleries built to include the enormous increase in worshippers. Yet the Puritans never suceceded in making public worship a civil obligation. They did succeed in stopping ordinary work, but never succeeded in stopping sports. Sunday did become a day of rest from labour, but even Cromwell's government refused to force people to church. The Act of Uniformity of 1682 and its consequent, the Toleration Act of 1689, destroyed the Tudor and Stuart concept that the Church of England embraced all the nation, but the proper observance of the Sabbath as a day that should be devoted to the worship of God survived until comparatively recent times. Throughout the eighteenth and nineteenth centuries it was generally accepted that the Sabbath was a sacred day and those who desecrated it did so at their own risk.

FOUR

The Flame of the Spirit

T. H. L. PARKER, in his study of Calvin draws attention to Calvin's fondness for two images, that of the 'labyrinth' and that of the 'schoolmaster'. Calvin was not an imagist writer, being much more a conceptual thinker with a great facility for communicating ideas in clear precise prose with dignity, but without pomposity. He has been called the father of French prose, and his style, both in French and Latin, was of no small importance in the growth of his influence as a theologian. His frequent use of the two images mentioned above may tell us more about him than they would if they had been used by a writer with a more poetic imagination. The use of the image of the 'schoolmaster' is understandable in a biblical scholar, since it is used in Scripture in defining the position of the law in relation to Christian commitment. 'The law is a schoolmaster to bring us to Christ', says St Paul, and this image would certainly commend itself to one who was all his life a teacher. Yet the image of the 'labyrinth' is not biblical, but belongs to pre-Christian pagan, and particularly Hellenistic, thought and legend. There was, of course, the famous labyrinth of Egypt, one of the Seven Wonders of the World, but from the manner in which Calvin uses the image in the first Book of the Institutes, it is far more likely that he had, subconsciously perhaps, in his mind the legend of Theseus who penetrated the labyrinth at Knossos and slew the Minotaur, guided in his adventure by the thread given to him by Ariadne.[1] The legend of Theseus focuses on an aspect of the Hellenic character overshadowed by the contemplative calmness of Plato, a character or mentality which was adventurous, searching, courageous and militant; a mentality which gave energy to a

[1] T. H. L. Parker, *Portrait of Calvin*, p. 50.

small nation to conquer and master for a time the known world, and which contains within itself the idea of nerve, of challenge, of man against the elements, of man who could face the terror of Scylla and Charybdis, the monstrosity of the giant Polyphemus, the seductiveness of the Sirens, and by sheer courage and tenacity return home in one piece, or bring back the prize of the Golden Fleece! It is not without significance that the historian should attribute the failure of the Greek experiment to failure of nerve, because it was nerve that made them an empire. A small nation set on expansion needs nerve more than any other quality, so a small man set on achievement and having to face the competition of those who start with vast resources in their hands, needs the nerve of a sense of destiny to sustain and support him. This sense of destiny Calvin found in the Scriptures 'those whom He foreknew to them He gave the destiny to be conformed to the image of His Son', and the man whom God foreknew and was given this destiny was the 'elect man', the man chosen by God for the manifestation of His Glory. This destiny was not determined by God's foreknowledge of merit but by the foreknowledge of whom He would choose to live; a gift entirely gratuitous to the elect, and for no reason save that it pleased God so to choose.

The image of the labyrinth pictures man lost in a maze with no plan or direction to lead him out of it, and represents in one sense the mind of man in its natural state. The image could be applied to the doctrine of predestination itself and particularly to those who fell into the trap of 'speculation', an attitude which Calvin particularly disliked. 'The election of God,' he says, 'is hidden and secret in itself but the Lord manifests it by the calling. Wherefore men are being fantastic or fanatical if they look for their salvation, or the salvation of others, in the labyrinth of predestination, instead of keeping to the way of faith which is offered to them.'[2] In the opening chapters of the Institutes, the image of the labyrinth is used in a much more subtle fashion. It really picks up the feeling of lostness which Calvin found, as he, a great humanist scholar, sought for God, and followed the tracks of humanity as it sought for God in the vast speculations of

[2] J. Calvin, *Commentary on John*, 6:40, Opp. 47, 147, and *Inst.* III, 21, 1.

human reason as to the meaning of life and its true goal. Francis Thompson fled Christ 'through the labrynthine ways' of his own mind, and Calvin came to see that this was what he was doing under the guise of seeking Him. Men, searching for some way to extricate themselves from their human bewilderment lost themselves in this maze, and in sheer pride or desperation made idols to worship whereby they worshipped not God but a figment of their own brain in His stead. Despite all their brilliance men were puzzled creatures, some becoming satisfied with the idolatry of their own solutions, others in despair sinking into a slothful agnosticism, but all caught in the built-in obsolescence of sin which predicated by its own nature a failure of achievement. Nothing could rescue men from this state unless it came from outside. Calvin found the 'thread' that rescued him in the Word, 'The Light of the Divine Countenance', which, the Apostle himself says, 'no man can approach unto' is like an 'inexplicable labyrinth to us, unless we are directed by the thread of the Word'.[3]

The 'thread' of the Word, however, does not come from nowhere to rescue the faithful—out of the blue as it were—it is given, as was the thread that guided Theseus. The giver is God, but the maker and communicator is the Holy Spirit. Everything that the elect man has in His gift; He inspired the prophets and the Apostles and they spoke by His power.[4] Men are elected, justified, sanctified, and glorified by His work in their hearts. It was the Holy Spirit that illuminated the Scriptures as their guide, and it was the Holy Spirit who communicated the life of Christ to the believer, and, with it all, the benefits received from the Father. Calvin is never tired of repeating that the Holy Spirit is the bond, as it were, by which the Son of God unites us to Him effectively.[5] Again it was the Holy Spirit, which, in the organism of the Church, the body of Christ, assigned to each member his place and function. Faith itself was a gift of the Holy Spirit to the elect man, for election was the mother of faith and not the reward of faith. Calvin was a convinced trinitarian attributing to the Father the commencement of every action and the source

[3] J. Calvin, *Institutes*, Book I, ch. 4, 3.
[4] Ibid., ch. 6, 3.
[5] Francois Wendel, *Calvin*, p. 239.

and origin of all things; to the Son the Wisdom and the order in which things are disposed; and to the Holy Spirit the virtue and efficacy of all actions.[6]

The 'thread' of the Word illuminated by the Spirit and confirmed by His inward testimony was not just a guide line for cautious self-preservation, but a life-line for adventurous living. The energy for this active holiness was the gift of the Holy Spirit to the believer in the Church. This was the philosophy which lay behind the concern of the Puritan for effectual righteousness; this is what nerved them for their activity, both personal and social; this is what gave two small nations, Holland and England, the courage to build great empires in the teeth of Spain's opposition. The work of the Holy Spirit in men, in the Church, and in society is of paramount importance in any appreciation of Puritan spirituality. This work was the constant theme underlying their preaching, so much so that they were often called 'the spiritual preachers' in contradistinction to the more scholastic preaching of other clergy, and spiritual preaching was the assessment of man in a spiritual context as the primary milieu in which his present work and future hopes were to be judged.

Man, to the Puritan, was not only a 'spiritual creature', he needed also to be a 'creature of the Spirit'. He was 'a spiritual creature' because he was a man of two worlds, the world of the flesh and the world of the spirit. Man possessed something more than a natural body, he possessed a rational soul which distinguished him from the animal creation and gave him dominion over the animal world. This did not mean that he could treat the animal world or the natural world as he liked, for his God-given authority carried with it duties and responsibilities. He could use the world but not for his own aggrandisement or selfish interests, but only for the glory of God. To do 'earthly things with a heavenly mind' is a phrase often used by the Preachers, and it implies that just because God has given man the special gift of a spiritual character, he must act always in accordance with the divine destiny conferred upon him in that special gift. The destiny that God had projected for men was that they were 'called to be Saints', the citizens of Heaven. In the Bible was

[6] J. Calvin, *Institutes*, Book I, ch. 13, 18.

spelled out the character of a Saint, and the function of the Church was to remind men of this spiritual nature and to convey such helps as God had ordained for them to achieve this sanctity.

But, while the Puritans believed that man was a spiritual creature, they were also very conscious of the fact that he was a creature of the flesh, and was, to use a phrase of Heidigger, 'living towards death'. This death to the Puritan was not just the final end of life, but the constant state in which men lived day by day. Of course, the natural man, even if he acknowledged that he was a spiritual creature, did not realize that he was totally committed to the flesh. It was part of the illusion under which he lived that he could do acts which had real merit in them, merit not only before men, but before God. This to the Puritan was all part of the vanity of human dreams and aspirations, for even religion could be vanity and, like that of the Scribes and Pharisees, just a form without power. Consequently, the Puritan asserted that submission to the flesh was the cause of man's alienation from God, the sin which subsumed all sins, for it was a tacit denial of the reality of the spiritual world. Such a man, sunk in selfishness and spiritual sloth, moved with the flow of time without hope to his appointed end; the Saints, on the other hand, caught glimpses of eternity, signals of transcendence, to encourage them on their way. These glimpses of eternity, these signals of transcendence, were the gifts of the Holy Spirit to man, and to those who responded to these signals was given also the power to live the life that they implied.

Man, therefore, not only needed the knowledge that he was a spiritual creature, he needed also to become a creature of the Spirit; that is, recreated by the Spirit, since he could not of himself live the spiritual life that God demanded of him.

The work of the Holy Spirit in the heart of man began right at the beginning of his calling to demonstrate by his life and witness the glory of God. It was the Holy Spirit who was the agent of God in election and reprobation.[7] The Spirit was a free gift, and, as Preston says, there is nothing more free than a gift, for a gift is to be received as a gift, it is given not because we deserve it. It is not drawn from God by force, nor merited

[7] John Preston, *Saint's Spiritual Strength* (The Saint's Qualifications), p. 170.

by works, all the good that is in the believer is given by God and it is He who puts the first stamp of holiness in man by the free gift of the Spirit. Because the Spirit is free, as God's agent in salvation He is free to choose whom He will save. He might have chosen Esau and not Jacob, for there cannot be a reason given why He should choose one and not the other. So He might choose the wife and not the husband, the child and not the father. He is free to choose or choose not, and the chosen one is the elect one, and the elect are Spirit filled men.

This consciousness of being the object of God's special providence was not exhausted in personal piety, but nerved men of the Elizabethan age to challenge the might of Spain and Portugal, in extending England's influence in the New World. The narratives gathered by Hackluyt of these predatory voyages abound with this consciousness. This even extended to the slavery expeditions of men like Sir John Hawkins. The Registrar of the voyage made by Sir John Hawkins in 1564 was John Sparke, and it was he who wrote an account of the voyage carrying slaves from Africa to the West Indies. They were becalmed for eighteen days, and as their store of water and food gradually diminished, they and their cargo were facing possible starvation, but God, 'who never suffers the elect to perish' sent a breeze which stayed with them all the journey until they reached the Cannibal Isles.[8] The elect were certainly not the negroes clamped in the holds, but the Christian Englishmen under the special providence of God! All the Elizabethans were conscious of living in a great age, an age in which divine providence had a special care for Englishmen. As Raleigh wrote to his dying Queen: 'I throw away my present honour and future, not as things of no value, but to bear witness to what I believe is truth; that to have lived in this age, your age, madam, is sufficient unto itself.' Part of the dynamic of that age was the consciousness of election. As A. L. Rowse says: 'It is fairly indicative that the greatest seamen, Drake and Hawkins were touched by the Puritan spirit.'[9]

But the Holy Spirit in chosing the elect did not do so without reference to Christ. He chose them in Christ, and no one could possess the Spirit without knowing Christ. The knowledge of

[8] Hackluyt's *Voyages*, Vol. 7, p. 20.
[9] A. L. Rowse, *The England of Elizabeth*, p. 466.

Christ was 'the oil wherein the flame of the Spirit lies',[10] and to know Christ was to possess His Spirit. Consequently, the elect man had to use the thread of the Scriptures to know Christ. The believer must therefore study the Scriptures continually to build up his knowledge of Christ, 'to be trading therein, to be busied in speaking, or reading, or in thinking therein!'[11] Every man must bestow his time on something, and most men spend their time on riches, or power, or chasing happiness in the lusts of the flesh. Yet none of these things brought happiness, only the knowledge of Christ could do that, and the Spirit which comes with the knowledge. So the believer as he faces strongholds that Satan has built up in the deceits and errors of the world and also in his own soul could attack them by his own spiritual insights, yet without success. He could go it alone without the Holy Spirit and fail, but Christ had provided the Spirit, the Holy Spirit, not only to convince the world of sin, of righteousness, and of judgement, but to sanctify men, so that they could fight, possessed of the whole armour of God.[12] But before the spiritual man was able to fight in the armour of the Spirit by his knowledge of Christ, there was a certain pre-condition, he had to recognize his status as in bondage to the law, for the law was a schoolmaster to bring him to Christ, and his bondage was the knowledge of his failure to obey this law. 'You may have the law opened to you a hundred times, that is the particular sinnes of which a man is guilty described, yea the particular judgements, yea the Lord may follow you with afflictions and crosses, but except there be the spirit of bondage to work together with these, it will never mollifie an abdurate heart.'[13] The spirit of bondage led to fear, fear of the just judgements of God. 'Therefore my beloved,' says Preston, 'if you have never been affrighted with the terror of God, if you have never been put into any feare by this spirit of bondage, be assured that you have not the spirit of Adoption.'[14] And yet those who had tasted this spiritual bondage brought about by failure to obey the law, and their knowledge

[10] John Preston, *New Covenant* (1629), p. 202.
[11] Ibid., p. 210.
[12] Ibid., p. 209.
[13] Ibid., p. 163.
[14] Ibid., p. 163.

of better things should not find it a just cause of dejection. It is a sign that God is beginning a good work in them, the good work of forgiveness, justification and sanctification. Therefore men should use their misery to bring them home to Jesus Christ. Having come to Christ they would receive the flame of the Spirit. So John Cotton writing to Archbishop Ussher to explain his views on God's 'eternal predestination' says that 'he dare not preach the Gospel indifferently to all, before the law, nor the worth of Christ, before the need of Christ'.[15] The concept of predestination and election was merely a framework for preaching God's mercy in that despite the condemnation of men in Adam, the archetypal man, God did choose some to life in Christ, His elect Son, the only one in whom He was well pleased. Having brought them to Christ they received the gift of Christ's Spirit that they might be sanctified as He was, and shine as flames of light in a dark and desolate world.

The strong emphasis that the Puritan Preachers laid on the work of the Holy Spirit had a correlative, for it was not enough to convince their hearers that the theological model of conversion, repentance, justification, sanctification, and glorification was true, they had also to try to show how a man could identify whether he possessed the Spirit or not. The test or signs that the believer was encouraged to look for can be summed up for us by John Preston in his treatise on spiritual death and life which was published under the title *An Elegant and Lively Description of Spiritual Life and Death.* 'The life of the Spirit begins when the Gospel is preached, and the Spirit kindles light on the heart to apprehend Gospel truth'.[16] This is where the Puritan Preacher started, the gift of the Spirit comes to a man in the preaching of the Word. Preston re-iterates the same sign in the *Saint's Spiritual Strength.* 'Did you receive the Spirit by the preaching of the Word?' he asks. This was the place where the Spirit was first given, because the first work of the Spirit was to stir up men to attend to the voice of Christ. Having brought men to attend to the voice of Christ it was the Spirit which kept

[15] C. R. Elrington (ed.), *Works of Archbishop Ussher*, Vol. 15, p. 331 (1864).

[16] John Preston, *An Elegant and Lively Description* (1632), p. 97.

[17] John Preston, *Saint's Spiritual Strength* (1637), p. 145.

the voice of Christ continually in the heart. For the function of the Spirit was to apply the general knowlege of faith, which all have who live in the Church, to particular believers. The general knowledge of faith, he says, is speculative, but to hear the voice of the Son of God is experimental.[18] The purpose of the work of the Spirit is to give men the knowledge that comes from the continual experience of listening to Christ in His Word.[19] This experimental knowledge produces the fear of God's judgement on the one hand, and the desire to know Him better on the other hand. It makes men 'approve and justify the ways of God to man',[20] so that no persecution or affliction can quench the holy joy that comes to a man when he has this experimental knowledge of Christ as Saviour. His affections are always towards God, and that must lead to action, for affections lead to action. 'If you are doers as well as hearers, the voice of Christ has spoken in you.'[21] Having made a conscience of hearing the Word, a man must take the Word as the voice of God and not of man. It is this that brings a man in conjunction with God the giver of spiritual life. 'For God is to the soul, what the soul is to the body. It is He by His Spirit which puts life in the soul.'[22] Particular actions must agree with the Word, and to do this man must 'conclude with God in prayer, let Him not deny you. One word from Him is worth a thousand from us.'[23] The Spirit therefore was above all else the 'Doctor of the Soul',[24] for it was He who taught men the true significance of the Word that lies within the Word, and enabled them to discern the signals of transcendence implanted in the soul of the believer.

But, while the concept of the Spirit as teacher and witness may be described as the more passive work of the Spirit even though it led to action and holy activity, there was a more active roll given to the Spirit by the Preachers which took place first of all in the soul and secondly in the intensity of the activity generated by the Spirit. A sure sign of knowing whether a man had

[18] John Preston, *An Elegant and Lively Description*, p. 97.
[19] Ibid., p. 99.
[20] Ibid., p. 104.
[21] Ibid., p. 109.
[22] Ibid., p. 122.
[23] Ibid., p. 129.
[24] John Preston, *The Saint's Spiritual Strength*, p. 154.

received the gift of the Spirit was by his manner of working; that is: was there a continual combat in the believer between the flesh and the Spirit? For, as St Paul said, 'the flesh lusteth against the Spirit and the Spirit against the flesh' (Gal. 5:17).

'If you have the Spirit you will have a continual fighting and striving in the Soule, and this will not only be against one, or some more particular lust, but against all that it knows to be Sin.'[25] This emphasis on the spiritual battle in the soul of the believer was nothing new, it is to be found in all the lives of the Saints in some form or another. The Puritan Preachers revived this emphasis as a sign of the possession of the Spirit. The natural man might suppress his lusts out of self-respect, as it were, but this was different from hating sin with all his heart, so that he fought against it with courage, by the supernatural aid of the Spirit. 'You will fight, but faintly, against sin except you have the Spirit.'[26] This demands a strict and continual self-examination of a man's own inclinations and temptations. 'Examine yourselves, what power you have when you pray, what power you have to go through to the end . . . when you are offered the profits and pleasures of the world, what power you have to forsake them if this prove hurtful to the inward man.'[27] The Spirit was given with power to aid, to comfort, and to bless, but above all to fight, and to fight with the assurance of victory. The gift of the Spirit was the gift of a strength above nature, for the Spirit adds holiness to the natural virtues as an end and aim of the Christian life, and this created a war between the nature of the self-centred, pleasure-loving, flesh, and the demands of a dedicated life which seeks only God's glory in righteousness, joy and peace. It is only when man hates sin and by the power of the Spirit seeks to conquer sin that he can have true contentment. The struggle was there, but the contentment of loving and pleasing God and God alone was there, too. 'Let a man look back to former times before he was called and see whether he ever found so much contentment in anything as he doth now.'[28] Even if he sins after his calling, he must not despair, but come home by

[25] Ibid., p. 154.
[26] Ibid., p. 155.
[27] Ibid., p. 155.
[28] John Preston, *Paul's Conversion*, p. 187.

'the weeping crosse',[29] which the Spirit in Christ has provided for him.

The most important sign, however, by which a man might know that he possessed the Spirit, was what Preston calls 'zeale'. It was the burden of much of the sermon he preached before the House of Commons exhorting them to be zealous for holy things and holy causes. 'Zeale is nothing else', he says, 'but the intention of all holy affections and holy actions.'[30] It is the act by which formality in religion is turned into affection for religion, a kind of spiritual heat which God gives to those who are baptised 'with the Spirit and with fire'. When the Apostles were so baptised at Pentecost they spoke with new tongues, so that the audience understood them. 'Ask yourselves', he says, 'are you cold in prayer, in love for the fellowship of other Christians in the Church, in speaking about holy things and experiences.' It is the property of the Spirit to heat the soul so that a man can say with the Prophet: 'The zeale of thine house hath eaten me up.' A man filled with this zeale for religion cannot see Christ dishonoured, nor the Church neglected and despised, nor holiness and goodness denigrated. Not to be hot in this way was to be luke-warm, which was odious to God. Such men were like the Laodiceans, and it was of these that God said in His Word that He would 'spew them out of His mouth'. This zeale for God was what ultimately saved men, for it was demonstrated by a hatred and loathing of sin, and a desire to do good. Not all men had this zeale, though they had a Christian faith. They were like Hannibal of whom it was said that he had a fire in him but it wanted blowing. Zeale to the Puritan, and this was the character given by Ben Jonson to the Puritan of *Bartholomew Fair*, was what 'enthusiasm' was for Wesley. For the world always did call those who expected a daily growth in their religion, by the grace and mercy of God, by the name of 'enthusiasts'. 'Zeale' or 'enthusiasm' was rightly applied to all who were saved from formal and nominal Christianity.[31] Associated with zeale as a mark of possessing the Spirit was also the certainty that if a man possessed the Spirit then he would do more than was

[29] Ibid., p. 286.
[30] John Preston, *Sermon before the House of Commons*, p. 264
[31] John Wesley, *Forty Four Sermons* (1964), p. 428.

normally expected of a Christian man. 'To do more' than he was expected was also a sign of possessing the Spirit, and by 'doing more' Preston did not only mean doing more by one's own personal growth in grace and love of the Church, it also included the good of mankind. This total activist stand could not prevail in the sluggish soul of man unless and until he possessed the gift of the Spirit. When he became conscious of possessing the Spirit, he was turned from a passive, cold, though perhaps pious individual, into a contentious one. 'Contend for the faith once delivered to the Saints' was the primary duty of those who sat in Parliament, so Preston told the House of Commons. It was to these men he appealed, the leaders in the community, the Lawyers of Lincoln's Inn, the gathered congregation of dons and students who listened to his preaching in Cambridge. In fact, if men in this position did not use their opportunities for serving the Lord, God would not accept what they did offer, just as a landlord would not accept from a tenant less than the whole rent due. 'Strive and contend for the advancing of Christ's Kingdom, the furtherance of the Gospel, for the good of mankind, for the flourishing of the Church, wherein our own good consisteth . . . contend with God in prayer, with our superiors by entreating, with our adversaries by resistance, with cold and luke-warm men by stirring them up.'[32] This is what zeale, the first mark of the Spirit led men into, even into 'revolutionary violence'.[33]

Yet, despite the possibility of an anarchic liberty inherent in the possession of the Spirit, an anarchy towards the Church and its 'ordinances' which flourished during and after the Civil War, Jacobean Puritanism as expressed by men such as John Preston, Richard Sibbes, and William Gould was church-orientated. Men had to see the possession of the Spirit through the life of the Church. They would have been horrified by George Fox's remark, 'if there was no Scripture for our Men and Women's Meetings, Christ is sufficient'.[34] Once the Spirit had been received by the preaching of the Word, His Presence was sustained by the frequent use of the ordinances of the Church, the study of the

[32] John Preston, *The New Covenant*, p. 560.

[33] Christopher Hill, *Puritanism and Revolution*, p. 253.

[34] George Fox, *Epistles*, p. 388.

Scriptures, and the fellowship of believers. There is no mention of the possibility of the 'charismata' in such phenomena as speaking with tongues and healing. These were special gifts needed for a time in the establishment of the Church, but not relevant apparently for that day and age, as they are never mentioned. The Preachers were in the broad stream of Christian theology which sought its doctrine of the Holy Spirit in the whole teaching of the Bible and not in an odd text or so. In doing so they came to emphasize certain theological truths which had a special reference to the life of salvation in the work of the Spirit in the soul of man, and were the first to articulate the 'Plan of Salvation' which in the two following centuries became the heart of evangelical preaching in this country. Another age no doubt needs another emphasis, and if the charismatic movement is a 'mighty protest against the determinate forms of the Church's existence in the world', as Professor Torrance asserts,[35] it might equally well be that this movement is the Protestant assertion of the Sovereignty of God, a demonstration of the Deity, over against the rationalist triumphalism of scientific disciplines, and parallels as it were, the increasing creation of Roman Catholic Saints during the last hundred years. In both cases the Deity is demonstrated by the miraculous. To the Puritan Preacher the miraculous was the conversion of a man from a life of sin to a life of holiness, and his persistence in pursuing the vision of God vouchsafed to him in that experience. This was the work of the Spirit.

[35] T. F. Torrance, *The Church in the New Era of a Scientific and Cosmological Change.*

FIVE

Plotting for Eternity

CHRISTOPHER Hill, in an illuminating analysis of John Preston's political sermons, draws attention to the use of the word 'plot', when Preston urges the need of prayer and fasting 'when there are great enterprises in hand, when there is anything "plotting" for the advancement of the good of the Church'.[1] In a note he also draws attention to Richard Sibbes, a friend and contemporary of John Preston, who uses the phrase 'we must plot for eternity' in a sermon preached at Great St Mary's, Cambridge, to commemorate the Anniversary of the Gunpowder Plot. It is perhaps an odd word to use in a sermon, yet the Jacobean age was, of course, very conscious of 'plots', very conscious of being poised a little uncertainly between the two poles of Protestant and Catholic power, with sincere and dedicated men seeking to control the centre of power, in the interest of one or other of these forces. Many could remember the execution of the handsome and popular Earl of Essex for plotting against Queen Elizabeth. Having at one time been her lover, there was tragedy and romance in the affair. All knew the story, current after the Queen's death, how she had given Essex a ring, saying, that if ever he was in trouble to send her the ring, and she would rescue him; and how she waited after his arrest for the ring, while her proud lover in the Tower obstinately refused to beg for mercy, and how at last she signed his execution order. Some would also remember Archbishop Bancroft's attack on the Puritan leadership late in Elizabeth's reign, and especially the books he had published,[2] in which he had tried to prove that

[1] Christopher Hill, *Puritanism and Revolution* (Puritan History), p. 252.

[2] R. Bancroft, *Dangerous Positions, A Survey of the Holy Disciples.*

the Puritans had plotted against Church and State. The Gunpowder Plot only served to heighten the consciousness that it was a 'plotting' age, and, after the discovery and the execution of the plotters, special prayers were included in the Prayer Book to commemorate November the 5th. Special sermons were preached on that day, and people were encouraged to celebrate their deliverance with bonfires and the burning of Guy Fawkes. Every year the people were reminded on plotting.

Politically the Gunpowder Plot put an end to the overt attempts of extreme Catholics to replace the Monarch with someone more favourable to their cause. It did not, however, stop 'plotting', and these various efforts to propagate the Catholic or Protestant cause in the Jacobean period centred not on the overthrow of the Monarch, but on the control of policy by backing one Favourite or another. The Catholics were in a favourable position because King James was determined to make peace with Spain, and to crown his peace policy by the marriage of his son, Prince Charles, to the Spanish Infanta. Everyone knew of the King's predilection for handsome youths, and the pro-Spanish party at Court, led by the Catholic Howards, had achieved great influence over the King by backing a young handsome Scotsman, named Robert Carr, as the King's Favourite. It was even on the cards that Carr, created the Earl of Somerset, would take over the negotiations for the marriage from the British Ambassador in Madrid. The anti-Spanish Puritan party at Court, led by Archbishop Abbott, and the Earls of Montgomery and Pembroke, decided to try to scotch this move by inserting a Protestant Favourite instead of Robert Carr, who would be under their influence and take directions from them. They noticed that James was becoming tired of Carr, who had recently got married, and the King was beginning to resent the arrogance of the Howard faction. They also knew that James, when hunting in the winter, had been introduced to a poor but handsome youth named George Villiers, and seemed attracted to him. Archbishop Abbott describes in his *Narrative* how the plot to substitute Villiers for Carr was accomplished. An entertainment was arranged at Baynards Castle, the town house of the Earl of Montgomery, for the Archbishop, the Pembrokes, the Hertfords, the Bedfords, and their retainers, where it was decided to back Villiers. 'One nail (as the Proverb is) having to be driven out by another.'[3] The key person to convince was the Queen, as James never took a male lover except on the Queen's recommendation, so that if she eventually complained, he could say that it was on her advice he had acted! The Queen took some persuading, but in the end she recommended George Villiers to the King, who knighted him and gave him an income of £1,000 per year. There was no holding Villiers back. He soon ousted Robert Carr, and within a few years was created Duke of Buckingham, and acted as the first minister of the King. The Puritan plot succeeded, as Buckingham took over the negotiations for the Spanish Marriage with the intention of frustrating it, which he succeeded in doing, and the Prince married the daughter of the French King.[4] It was by the influence of the Duke of Buckingham that John Preston was made a Chaplain to Prince Charles and a Court Preacher, and for a time he was high in the councils of the Duke with the other Puritans such as Lord Saye and Sir John Eliot. Urbane, sauve and dedicated John Preston plotted for the advancement of the Church as he and the Puritan Party understood it.

The use of the word 'plotting' by John Preston in regard to the advancement of the Church, and the use of the same word in regard to the soul's salvation by his friend Richard Sibbes, illustrates the fact that there was no real distinction in the Puritan mind between politics and religion. When a man plotted for the advancement of the Church he was plotting for eternity, for the Church was eternity in time. Or as John Preston puts it, 'God is not only an habitation unto His Church, from generation to generation, but also from everlasting to everlasting.'[5]

Consequently, Puritan thought moved easily between personal salvation and the good of the Church. They were both part of the operation of Grace. It was by Grace that the elect were chosen, through the power of the Holy Spirit, and they were the Church. To say that Preston failed 'to distinguish between

[3] Archbishop Abbott's *Narrative*, Rushworth Coll. (1721), Vol. 1.

[4] Irvonwy Morgan, *Prince Charles's Puritan Chaplain*, ch. 5.

[5] John Preston, *Breastplate of Faith and Love* (The Eternity of God), p. 171.

politics and religion',[6] is to read back a twentieth-century attitude into the Puritan mind. It may be that the twentieth century distinction between politics and religion is a right distinction, but it has little relevance to the Puritan mind, for to them political action was merely an instrument of religion, and like every other activity of life would pass away as all things pass away. Only God, the soul, heaven and hell were eternal. What a man loved today, he would not love tomorrow: 'therefore', says Preston, 'love them not, regard them not, for they are of flitting and passing nature, but he that doeth the Will of the Lord abides for ever.'[7] On the other hand, Grace reached to eternity, and sin reached to eternity, so these were the two things men should be busied about. In all Puritan thought there is a strong consciousness of the vanity of earthly things, the shortness of earthly days, the foolishness of trusting in man. All things had an end, and man was no exception, he too was hurrying to the 'West of his dayes'. Christopher Hill quotes a moving passage from one of Preston's sermons, which illustrates the vanity of human effort: '. . . plainly we may see if we take it into consideration, mankind hurried along to the West of his dayes . . . our fathers have gone before, and we are passing, and our children shall follow at our heels, that as you see the billowes of the sea, one tumble on the neck of another, and in the end all are dashed upon the shoare; so all generations and ages in the end are split on the bankes of death, and thus is the condition of every man.' But Dr Hill omits the consequent of this sonorous passage, namely, 'Is it not our wisdom then to provide for another life.'[8] Such passages were not spoken from a general philosophical impersonal dissertation on the futility of life, but as part of the pressure to urge men to plot for eternity. So, indeed, were Preston's 'political' sermons. When preaching before Charles I in 1625, just before Buckingham's ill-fated expedition to the Isle of Rhé, he urges the King to help the Reformed Churches on the Continent, by arguing that God had made a Covenant with His people, and if His Covenant was not kept the country would come under the wrath of God.

[6] Christopher Hill, *Puritanism and Revolution*, p. 255.

[7] John Preston, *Breastplate of Faith and Love* (The Eternity of God), p. 16.

[8] John Preston, *Golden Sceptre* (1639), (The Cup of Blessing), p. 523.

But the Covenant was not made between God and the individual, or God and the Puritan party, or God and the Church even, but between 'God and us'. 'Between God and England.'[9] England was especially blessed and her favour with God demanded a Church-orientated political stance. 'We see all countreys round about us in confusion, and we (as it were the three young men in the fiery furnace) safe without so much as smooke or the smell of fire, as if we were the only people of God's delight.'[10] It is not a far cry from this to Milton's *Avimadversions* that God 'hath yet ever had this land under the speciall indulgent eye of His providence.' To the Puritan therefore Englishmen were in a special manner; 'God's Englishmen', their political actions should serve their Religion. By advancing the Church by political action they were plotting for eternity.

But, not only should men's political actions serve the eternal purpose of God in His Church, but men's personal lives should serve God's eternal purposes in their election to life. Right from the beginning of the world, says Richard Sibbes, there had been a 'continuall conspiracy of Satan and his instruments against God and goodnesse.'[11] Consequently, even the best of God's Saints were liable to be the subjects of the plots of wicked men. 'Emperors and Kings became Christians but Satan never yet became a Christian.' This arch-politician[12] was still plotting the destruction of man. But God had a plot still beyond Satan and his instruments. He had plotted man's redemption in Christ,[13] and in His Providence merely uses Satan and his minions, to be the executioners of His will. For it 'stood in His honour to outwit Satan and all wicked men.' He sometimes allowed Anti-Christ to make war with the Saints and overcome them. (Rev. 18) But even this did not discourage the Saints for by the help of the Spirit of God, the Saints knew themselves to be 'the conqurered people of God, but the people of God still'.[14]

In the day of God's judgement, the Saints would see all God's promises performed, all His threatenings executed, and all

[9] John Preston, *A Sensible Demonstration of the Deitie*, pp. 52–3.
[10] Richard Sibbes, *Saint's Cordialls* (1637), p. 157.
[11] Ibid., p. 143.
[12] Ibid., p. 148.
[13] Ibid., p. 151.
[14] Ibid., p. 147.

enemies trodden forever under the feet of Christ and His Church. Therefore the Saints must plot how to avoid Satan's plot, by remembering that their time was short, their talents many, their account short, the Judge impartial. The Saints must labour to be like their Judge who went about doing His Father's business and came to destroy the works of the devil. Their aim therefore was to be like the Ideal, the Pattern of all Grace, by whom they hoped to be saved; 'to bring forth good fruit to have opportunity, ability, and a heart to doe good'.[15] They should labour to be good in themselves and to do good to others for 'such as we are, such are our thoughts, such are our devices'.[16] This battle in the soul of man between Satan and Christ which demanded the co-operation of Saints in fighting to bring their desires and lusts under control was also an opportunity of plotting for eternity, for eternal life was man's proper objective and reward.

But this plotting for eternity was not the plotting of men to take or achieve a position they did not possess, but to defend and extend a position which was already theirs. The elect were already possessed of eternal life and walked with God and His Saints. It was even now 'the life of God and Angels, it is that life which we shall live hereafter'.[17] When Preston was dying he talked much before his death of the vanity and emptiness of all things here below and also of 'his own belief and expectation of a sudden change; not of my company (said he) for I shall still converse with God and His Saints, but of my place and manner of doing it'.[18] To the Puritan Preacher there was no difference in conversing with the Saints below and conversing with the Saints in heaven. The elect on earth and in heaven were one people separated by time and space, which in their turn would pass away. The one reality was God and His Church, for the Saints were 'hidden in Christ', they lived in the object of their affection and so 'they never die againe'.[19] Consequently,

[15] Ibid., p. 151.
[16] Ibid., p. 152.
[17] John Preston, *An Elegant and Lively Description of Spiritual Life and Death* (1632), p. 70.
[18] Clarke's *Martrologie Life of John Preston*, p. 112.
[19] John Preston, *An Elegant and Lively Description*, p. 26.

those who were not in Christ did not possess true life. They were dead men, 'walking ghosts', as Preston calls them, they were like apparitions that assume a formal body for a time and then you see them no more. The unregenerate act like men, see like men, pray like men, and they have a certain civility, but their end is self-centred pleasure or gain, and their appreciation of religion is pure formality. What they lacked is what the Saints possessed, the power of the Holy Spirit, for it is the Spirit that gives life. Yet, despite this stark contrast between those who possess eternal life and those who do not, between the Saints and the 'walking ghosts',[20] Preston appears to allow the faint possibility to his hearers that all is not lost, for even they may be of the elect. They should, therefore, try their luck, as it were, by repenting and using the ordinances which are the vehicles of the Spirit, recognizing that real repentance is brought about not by their own effort but by God's act alone. Only He breathes life into dead men, but not into all, only those He chooses. Consequently, it is wisdom to wait on the means of Grace in the ordinances of the Church, for through the means of Grace God will demonstrate their election. For instance, good motions may begin in you, press them forward, 'they are the offspring of life'.[21] Ask yourself seriously, 'am I dead or alive?', and if dead do not say to yourself 'it's not in my power to quicken, it is only in God to doe it, and he doeth this but in a few . . . how then shall I be in the number?' Give yourself no rest, know that it is God that breatheth, and then depend on Him. Make use of the doctrine of election, 'with care and more solicitude to looke to yourselves'.[22] The operative words are 'give yourself no rest'. Plotters for eternity were restless men, dissatisfied with their present condition, seeking happiness but not finding it. They were active men 'for action begets life and life begets action'.[23] They were men not content to let things take their course, not content to let the enemy triumph. If at times they began to languish in holy doing, then their remedy was to be up and doing. They should 'walk in the Spirit', for those who

[20] Ibid., p. 26.
[21] Ibid., pp. 33 and 34.
[22] Ibid., pp, 33 and 34.
[23] Ibid., p. 85.

have the Spirit, says Preston, 'stand not still as one that cannot stirre, this acting helps the spirit, first by enlarging and extending life, secondly by preventing that which increaseth death; the more we walk in the ways of life the more we prevent the way that leads to the chamber of death. Be doing, if not on one thing then another. In the stepping out of your callings, be doing, reading and praying; confessing and talking of good things. The neglect of this is cause why there are so many dwarfes in Grace'.[24] 'Christianity', says Richard Sibbes, 'is a busy trade.[25] Zeal and busyness about good works, united with faith and persistence in which you give 'God no rest' demanded resolute, determined, even violent men. 'If a Christian would resolve in the power of God to break through all difficulties and do all duties, God would second Him.'[26] 'He that would have the Kingdom of Heaven must use violence to take it.'[27] That is he must wrestle and strive against his appetites to keep them under; he must wrestle and strive with God in prayer to help him with fervency and persistence. 'Above all he must not let go of God whatever happens.'

If to give oneself no rest in plotting for eternity is a condition essential to the Christian life, then John Preston fulfilled it. When he died he must have gone straight to heaven! He must have lived in his carriage! Posting up to London to preach at Lincoln's Inn; posting back to Cambridge to lecture at Trinity Church, and in his College; down to Dorchester to consult with John White; off to Coventry to preach where he first met James Ussher, later Bishop of Armagh; moving about the Court, in and out of the Duke's private rooms 'with a fly audacity' at least three times a week, says John Heylin in his *Life of Archbishop Williams.* Calling in at the salon of the Duchess of Denbigh, sister of Buckingham, where he first met William Laud; travelling in secret to the Continent 'disguised as a gentleman'; visiting Catholic States, giving out that he was willing to be converted; calling on Elizabeth of Bohemia, James I's daughter in exile in the Hague from the Palatinate. Arrang-

24 Ibid., p. 86.
25 Richard Sibbes, *Saints Cordialls*, p. 386.
26 Ibid., p. 390.
27 John Preston, *Golden Sceptre*, p. 231.

ing a chaplain for her when he came home; rushing up to London for a consultation on Puritan affairs with Lord Saye; consulting the Duchess of Bedford; writing to Lady Vere to get a 'place' in the Church for Dr Wilson, negotiating liberty to preach again for Arthur Hildersham, or John Cotton; visiting Sir Richard Knightly at Fawsley Hall in the summer, and going to stay with John Cotton at Boston. Consulting John Dod. Meeting the London Puritan Conference regularly; draughting a letter to persuade Buckingham to stop the Spanish marriage,[28] but doing it incognito; 'Conceale me in this' is a phrase he often used in these 'plottings' for the good of the Church. He worked himself to an early death at 41 in the height of his powers, and if any one man rescued the Puritan Movement from the doldrums into which it had fallen in the last years of Elizabeth, and the first years of James I, it was John Preston. He moved swiftly from Court to country, from college to city, weaving a web of contacts anchored to the centre of political life, the Court and Parliament.

While John Preston in common with all the Godly Preachers emphasized in sermon after sermon that eternal life was a present possession of the elect, he also emphasized that the elect had to qualify for it! The qualification was to be elected and to be elected was to be 'in Christ', for God's eternal election of some to life, while passing others by, was election in Christ. Indeed, Calvin himself had said 'that if a man was in communion with Christ, he had clear proof that he was one of the elect', for Calvin equated the elect with believers and says 'did all promiscuously bend the knee to Christ election would be common'.[29] Consequently, the basic qualification for possessing eternal life in the existential moment is to be a believer. Richard Sibbes and John Davenport published a series of John Preston's sermons after his death under the title of *The Saint's Qualification* (1633), which set out the theological framework of such qualification. In the first edition there were ten sermons on 'Humiliation', nine sermons on 'Sanctification', and three sermons on 'Communion with Christ in the Sacrament'. These

[28] Irvonwy Morgan, *Prince Charles's Puritan Chaplain*, pp. 55–9.

[29] John Calvin, *Institutes of the Christian Religion*, H. Beveridge, Vol. 2.

sermons were re-issued again in 1634 and 1637, with additions such as a 'Heavenly Treatise of the Divine Love of Christ'; the 'Christian's Freedom'; the 'Deformed Form of a Formal Profession'; 'Christ's Fullness and Man's Emptiness'. The burden of this preaching may be summed up in Preston's own words: 'When God means to save a man, He will goe through with the worke, and never gives over till He hath brought him home—a smalle thing when God hath the working of it, shall worke, and never give over working, till our hearts be qualified aright, till we believe in Christ and embrace the Gospel.'[30]

God was a very determined person to the Puritan Preacher. He would not be defeated by the plots of Satan against goodness and righteousness, nor by the foolishness of men who preferred Satan's lordship to His own. God had created man to enjoy eternal life, but man had succumbed to Satan's wiles and become a rebel against God and His law. Those whom God had determined to save would be saved. When Francis Thompson described his own spiritual experience of being pursued by Christ in The Hound of Heaven, until he was cornered and driven to his knees with his armour of pride hewn from him piece by piece, he was describing in his own way a conviction of the Puritan that the elect man could not escape God. 'The Gospel', says John Preston, 'is a net that catches men, and as in the taking of fishes, if they will take the fish, they break the sides of the River, and will not suffer them to rest in any corner for if they can find any place to rest in they will not come into the net. So man hath many starting holes and faine would be quiet God humbles him a little, but he gets in a nooke and then hides himself, that if God beat not the River thorowout, that is if God doe not pursue a man, he will not be brought in.'[31]

The purpose of the pursuit is to humble men. A man cannot be justified by the righteousness of Christ until he has been humbled. Humiliation, therefore, precedes justification and sanctification. It was the work of the Holy Spirit in the heart to convince a man of sin, of righteousness and of judgement. This was as much a necessity to the elect as it was to the unregenerate, for the Puritan Preacher had no exalted opinion of the nature of

[30] John Preston, *Saint's Qualification* (1637), p. 21.
[31] Ibid., p. 22.

man. Two of Preston's sermons on 'Humiliation' bear the title, 'The Nature of Man is full of all Unrighteousness and Ungodliness', and with minute analysis he describes how the understanding of man is corrupted; how the will of man is the source of contrariness, pride, inconstancy and disobedience; how the memory of man, the conscience of man, the appetites of man are corrupted by the sin of Adam and by his own sin. This total corruption of man is demonstrated to man by the Spirit and the Word, so that man sees what he really is when confronted by the holiness of God as displayed in His law. Part of man's humiliation is the knowledge that he justly deserves God's wrath, and that he surely will be punished by God. And yet, this revelation of God's wrath is not without hope for it is revealed to man that he may go to Christ for succour and salvation, that he may lay the blame where it really lies, on himself and not on God, and that he might glorify God for His patience and long suffering. Nor is this humiliation a once for all affair. It is an attitude of mind and soul which is a permanent state. Consequently, a 'Saint must bring his heart to God every day—should call himself to a reckoning for every sin, for all sorts of omissions and commissions.'[32] The first qualification for possessing eternal life in Christ, is to be humbled at the knowledge of one's sins, to acknowledge the judgement deserved, and feel the need of Christ's mercy.

This grace of Humility before God's righteousness and judgement was one of the great underlying themes of Puritan preaching. But it was not meant to stand alone, as it were. This stance was necessary if a man was to receive God's Spirit and the life of heaven which God could give him. He had to learn to hate what the righteous God hated, and what the righteous God hated was sin. Now God hated sin not only because it was His Holy nature to do so, but because of the sorrow, pain and distress that sin brought to His children. He had created men to be the Temples of the Holy Ghost 'wherein God delights to dwell'.[33] So, in sixteen sermons why men should forsake sin,

[32] Ibid., p. 184.
[33] Ibid., p. 273.

Preston analyses the effect of sin on man's human nature,[34] which should lead him to repentance and a desire to be saved by Christ. Nor should men be backward in seeking this salvation for God is merciful 'therefore when you heare that Christ is exceeding mercifull, then come in; only lay down the arms of rebellion, and you shall find mercy'.[35] The end for which humiliation, repentance, conversion, justification and sanctification are designed, is that God's children should love Christ and love one another.

A second underlying theme of Puritan Preaching and a qualification for possessing eternal life was faith. 'Humiliation and faith', says Preston, 'are the two antecedents to knowing the love of the Lord Jesus.'[36] A man must be broken and moulded again before he can find the love of Jesus, but he knows and receives Christ by faith. Faith is not only an act of the mind to believe that God will pardon us, but of the will and of the heart also to take Christ. To receive Christ is the sum of the Gospel. It is the good news, for the Preacher offers men not forgiveness of sin, but the Lord Jesus, for when a man has received Christ by faith, all the promises are his. 'Just have Christ and have the promises belong to you, not before.'[37] In a *Soliloquy of a Devout Soule to Christ*, Preston asserts that 'it is faith that appropriates Christ to the believing soule, but it is a faith that works by love.'[38] 'Hitherto I have loved thee', says he, 'but for lust not love; I would have thee save me, but I would not honour and please thee . . . thou has often shewed me thy riches, and I have loved them, but shew me thy selfe, that I may love thee.'

The object of faith therefore is to know Christ and to live in Him by love. It is to sit with Christ in Heaven now and to sit as judges so that if any sin arise to accuse or condemn, it must be with your votes'.[39] 'As Paul triumphed', says Thomas Goodwin,

[34] Ibid., pp. 271–88.
[35] Ibid., p. 294.
[36] John Preston, *A Heavenly Treatise of Divine Love* (Sermon I), p. 6.
[37] Ibid., p. 6.
[38] John Preston, *Saint's Qualification* (A Soliloquy of a Devout Soule to Christ), p. 90.
[39] Thomas Goodwin, *Works* (1862 Ed.), Vol. 4, p. 54.

'so must we; for at the present we sit in heaven with Christ, and have all our enemies under our feet.'[40] Thomas Goodwin describes in his spiritual biography how he was converted by John Preston's preaching.[41] He became one of the most decisive supporters of Independency in the Westminster Assembly, and Cromwell appointed him President of Magdalen College, Oxford. He edited, with Thomas Ball, Preston's Cambridge sermons. In a treatise setting forth Christ as the object of faith, based on the text, Romans 8:34, he begins by asserting that the text is a triumphant challenge uttered by the Apostles in the name of all the elect. It is they and they alone who enjoy in Christ eternal life now, and they know this by faith. This faith is not a mere looking at the tragic story of Christ's suffering and death, however much one's heart may be affected by it, but it is to apprehend the meaning of His death, and what was intended by it. Goodwin's explanation of this is that God 'plotted' man's salvation and Christ joined in this plot. It was not the malice of the Jews, the falseness of Judas, the fearfulness of Pilate, or the iniquity of the times he fell into, that wrought His death so much as God His Father complotting with Christ Himself and aiming at a higher end than they did.[42] It was by the 'determinate counsel and fore-knowledge of God' that Christ satisfied eternal justice, bore our sins on the tree and died in our stead. Faith should therefore look to this plot of God and Christ in His suffering to satisfy our sin and justify sinners. God accepted Christ's act and took Him to heaven in His resurrection and ascension to be there the Head of the Church. Therefore, all elect believers are in Christ in heaven, and are members of Christ. 'Christ therefore is our element, and He being ascended, we are sparks that fly upward to him.'[43] The Elect, therefore, are in communion with Christ and to remain in this communion in the power of the Spirit, in using all the means of Grace, in mortifying the flesh, in striving for perfect love, is the fundamental qualification for the possession of heaven and eternity now. Of course, it would not be easy for

[40] Ibid.
[41] Ibid., Vol. 2, Life.
[42] Ibid., Vol. 4, p. 19.
[43] Ibid., p. 54.

the Saint to live this heavenly life on earth. There would be fightings, fears, doubts, sorrows, chastenings and perhaps even despair, but the Saint had at least one confidence, for in the Gospel economy as far as he was concerned it was 'Mercy', says Goodwin, 'that manageth the plot'.[44]

[44] Ibid., p. 231.

SIX

Look for a Rainy Day

IF, as Jeroslav Pelikan asserts, the core of the Christian faith is a pessimism about life, and an optimism about God,[1] then the Puritan surely qualifies as an orthodox Christian. Life itself was under a curse, the curse of what the theologians called Original Sin, and every evil, physical and moral, was the consequence of man's first ancestral disobedience to God's commands. This awareness of evil was not confined to the thoughts and actions of man, for the result of the Fall was that man was no longer living in a friendly or even a neutral universe. The world itself was dominated by the victor in the garden so that Satan was not only the personification of all evil, but also the ruler of the world for a season under God's providential permission. The doctrine of the Fall of man, and its consequent the doctrine of Original Sin was *de fide*, as it were, to all Christians, because it was part of the revelation of God in Holy Scriptures. To the Puritan at least this was the ultimate authority, higher than that of Pope, Councils, Fathers of the Church, Men and Angels.[2] The Bible was God's document which put man in his place, and his place was that of a sinner doomed to destruction. The Scriptures contained 'nothing that pleaseth man'[3] except the free mercy of God for His Elect. But while the Puritan accepted the world-view of the Scriptures, and the mythology of the origin of sin offered there as an explanation of a mystery about life, he was much more concerned to emphasize the fact of sins, as displayed in such vices as hatred, envy, lust, pride,

[1] Jeroslav Pelikan, *The Shape of Death*, p. 5.
[2] C. S. P. D. Eliz., 5th June 1571.
[3] John Preston, *The Doctrine of Self-Denial* (1632), p. 98.

gluttony and cowardice, and so on. Men were activated by these emotions as they looked after their own selfish interests. There was a great deal of the 'Naked Ape' about men and they could and did behave like animals on occasions. On the other hand men had good qualities too, such as courage in adversity, a stoical acceptance of the 'slings and arrows of outrageous fortune'. Men could love, and could sacrifice themselves for others in love. But, taking it all in all, the 'bias' (a word John Preston often uses) in a man's nature was towards sin, and life itself brought afflictions which could overwhelm with temptation even the strongest.[4] Life was more difficult still for the Saints for they had stepped out, or been dragged out, of the ranks of natural man, to challenge the power of evil, and the very fact that they had 'stood up to be counted' drew Satan's wrath upon them as well as his malice. They were more overwhelmed by life than others, because the God whom they served allowed them to be afflicted, not only materially but spiritually. The natural man sunk in selfishness and sloth moved with the flow of time without hope to his appointed end. The Saints, on the other hand, caught glimpses of eternity, yet only to find that life with its trials and questionings, its fears and sorrows, its crosses and temptations, brought doubts as to the reality of the vision. The Preachers laboured with exegesis, illustration, syllogism and eloquence, to demonstrate that spiritual truths were the only reality, and that the finite world had a built-in obsolescence which no man could escape. The Saint seemed to be like a drowning man overwhelmed by the tide, who was advised to take comfort from the fact that there was land at the bottom . . . and that if only he could plant his feet on the land he could find that it was the land that was real and the turbulent seas an illusion! In the existential moment, of course, these afflictions both spiritual and physical were real enough, and the Saint had to be warned that afflictions would come, and come with greater force because he was committed to God's Cause. 'So', says John Preston, 'if you mean to follow Christ look for a rainy day; it may be that it is fair in the morning, but yet we know not what the evening

[4] John Preston, *The Golden Sceptre* (First Sermon on Humiliation), pp. 38–49.

will be—shall a man goe to sea and not look for storms—shall a soldier goe into the warres and not look for enemies?'[5]

The pessimism and optimism of Puritan spirituality revolved around the questions of certainties and doubts, and so the question 'In what can a man trust?' goes to the heart of Puritan preaching and gives it its special emphasis. Rarely does one find a sermon on the theme of Christmas such as delighted Lancelot Andrewes, or on the Apostles, except St Paul, and certainly not on the Canonized Saints of the Church. But there are hundreds of sermons on Humiliation, on Conversion, on the Gift and Workings of the Holy Spirit, on the Sovereignty of God, on the Effectual Calling of the Elect, the Nature of Sanctification, the Eventual Glory of the Saints, and the Privileges and Security of the Church. Yet, no hymn in all the hymnody of the Church expresses better the feel and temper of Puritan spirituality than Bernard of Cluny's great hymn which we know under the popular title of 'Jerusalem the Golden'. For though Bernard was a Catholic, he was also a monk, and a monk is a puritan at heart. Brief life, he says, is the portion of mankind, sorrow and care in this world. A wanderer on the earth, a sinner, a worm in the sight of God, yet, man was offered a hope, a mansion with the blessed of the ages in the New Jerusalem of God. In those bright halls all jubilant with song dwelt his Prince who had conquered and overcome the powers of evil. The Saint, too, could attain this victory, and see in Heaven his Prince face to face. Meanwhile, he had to watch and pray knowing that 'Zion in her anguish with Babylon must cope', but the certainty of attainment was there because the sweet and blessed country which was set forth as the objective of his existence was the home of God's elect. So the Saints were exhorted and encouraged to win that glory and they, though dust and ashes, could exult, for the Lord would be, and was even now their part. The Preachers of the great age of Puritain preaching, the Jacobean age, were concerned to assert the reality of this vision, and the worthwhileness of the struggle to attain this reality, while challenging the rising tide of Arminian humanism and the sceptical questing attitude of what came to be a secular and scientific approach to life. Whereas their contemporary, Francis

[5] John Preston, *The Doctrine of Self-Denial* (1632), p. 85.

Bacon, would say, 'If man begin with certainties he shall end in doubts, but if he will be content to begin with doubts, he shall end in certainties,'[6] they said a man must begin with certainties, the certainty of God and his own election to life. This does not exclude doubting, for doubting is something that resists faith, for where there is no faith there cannot be doubting.[7] But the certainty was there if a man trusted wholly in Christ, his Prince, and viewed the gaudy attractions of the world with the distrust and pessimism they deserved.

In the period we are considering, this sense of pessimism about life was enhanced by the apparent frustration of Puritan hopes. Under John Preston's leadership the Puritan movement had risen almost to the heights it had attained when it was patronized by the Earl of Leicester in the reign of Elizabeth I. For Preston under the Duke of Buckingham's patronage had been made free of the Court as Chaplain to Prince Charles. But this preferment was very much in the teeth of King James's opposition. The Scottish Earls at Court, the Dukes of Hamilton and Lennox, had failed to get Preston appointed Chaplain to the King. But the Duke of Buckingham, cultivating the young Prince Charles, had succeeded in adding the Puritan leader to the Prince's household. Yet James was still King and it was his policies which prevailed. James was determined to conclude a treaty with Spain, and entertained the idea that this could be part of an agreement for the marriage of Prince Charles to the Spanish Infanta. He was so concerned not to hinder this possibility that he seemed willing to sacrifice his daughter, Elizabeth, to this dream, since he persistently opposed any attempt to restore by force her husband's inheritance after the Elector had been driven out of the Palatinate into exile at the Hague, by the Spanish levies of Ferdinand of Austria. It seemed to the Puritan that Anti-Christ, namely, the Pope, and the Roman Church, was triumphing everywhere. The Puritan Preachers charged the Establishment with lack of 'zeale' in God's cause and looked back to the Elizabethan age where there was light, the light of the Reformation, and 'zeale'. England should 'stand in the gap' to

[6] Francis Bacon, *Advancement of Learning*, I., v. 8.

[7] John Preston, *Breastplate of Faith* (1630), (Of Effectual Faith), pp. 24–8.

preserve true religion and the integrity of the English nation, and come to the support of the 'kingdom of Grace abroad'.[8] Under the Gospel, England was preserved like 'Gideon's fleece', dry when all around was wet with blood.[9] Yet, the times were in danger of slipping away from the Gospel. Twice in a generation the Word had been barely saved, once in 1588[10] when the Armada was defeated, and again at the Gunpowder treason and plot. Even this did not warn the clergy or the Court. The approval shown by the Court for Richard Montague's books; the growth of Laud's influence; the pressure put on the Preachers, leading to the flight of many of them to the New World; the King's fear of Puritan Preachers who commanded the ear of the people;[11] the theatre's accusation of hypocrisy, muted in Shakespeare, open and blatant in Ben Jonson; the distinction between Puritan and Protestant made in some of the most popular pamphlets of the time,[12] though intended to encourage Puritans, also tended to increase this sense of isolation and frustration. It was as if Pelion was being piled on Ossa so that the normal pressures of life from which all men suffered were directly increased towards those who were trying to 'live godly'. The sermons of the time reflect this lack of confidence in earthly policies and rewards, and set over against them the all-sufficiency of God to sustain and ultimately glorify His people. But the fact that all Puritan Preachers encouraged the Saints to distrust the world, and look for true life in spiritual religion did not answer the question—'Why were the Saints afflicted?' Since the Saints were especially chosen of God why did they have to suffer? It was true that time and chance happened to all men, but this was beside the point in some respects, for the point was, in what way was the Saint, the elected one, different from ordinary man? The Preacher's answer was that the difference was not in the fact of adversity, but in his interpretation of its origin and meaning. Again and again John Preston contrasts the attitude of the civil man, as he calls him, and the Saint, to

[8] John Preston's sermon preached before the House of Commons.
[9] John Preston, *Golden Sceptre*, p. 47.
[10] Ibid., p. 279, and Thomas Goodwin's *Works* III, p. 158.
[11] Irvonwy Morgan, *Prince Charles's Puritan Chaplain*, pp. 151–3.
[12] Thomas Scott, *Vox Populi and Vox Regis*.

the vicissitudes of life, and the contrast has something in common with the different attitudes of the Stoic and the Christian to life. Adversity, suffering, crosses and afflictions were mysteries to all men, and all men tried to bridge these mysteries with some sort of plausibility. The 'civil man' could find that 'sweet are the uses of adversity',[13] and discover a 'jewel in the crown of the horned toad'. Nature could comfort him with 'adversities sweet milk philosophy'.[14] If God sent him the 'bread of adversity and the water of affliction',[15] at least there was bread and water there. That civil contemporary man, Francis Bacon, having progressed from the teachings of his godly puritan mother to the sweets of high office and the pleasures of the flesh, found, having lost his high office, that he could only philosophize on adversity and prosperity. Prosperity, he discovered, was the blessing of the Old Testament, adversity being the blessing of the New. So, 'prosperity doth then but discover vice, but adversity doth but discover virtue'.[16] But it was not his early Puritan teaching that he rediscovered, it merely gave a patina of religion to the philosophy of the civil man. Having a profound reverence for moral principles, Bacon yet chose invariably the course of self-interest; the aphorism 'a man that hath no virtue in himself ever envieth virtue in others'[17] arose as much from his knowledge of himself as it did out of contemplating his fellows. His Essays show a respect for and even love of justice, yet he perverted justice in the service of King James and the Duke of Buckingham both in the interest of his own fortune, and that of his aristocratic patrons. No doubt he conformed to the times with its high-flown principles, yet personal corruption; its separation of the pursuit of knowledge from the application of such knowledge to one's self; its neglect of truth, which, as Bacon says, 'only doth judge itself',[18] for the lie 'which faces God and shrinks from Man'.

If anyone has described what John Preston calls the 'civil man'

[13] William Shakespeare, *As You Like It* II, 1.12.
[14] William Shakespeare, *Romeo and Juliet* III, 3.4.
[15] Isaiah, 30 : 20.
[16] Francis Bacon, *Essays,* 'On Adversity' (Everyman), p. 15.
[17] Ibid., p. 24.
[18] Ibid., p. 4.

it is his contemporary, Bacon, who not only described him in brilliant language but exemplified him in his own nature. For Bacon, sophisticated, highly intelligent, ambitious, scholarly, and cultured, lacked the one virtue which lies at the root of religion, namely, humility. He certainly suffered great humiliations, falling from the height of Lord Chancellor of England to imprisonment in the Tower; fined an enormous fortune for accepting bribes; banned for ever from sitting in Parliament, he drank to the dregs the cup of adversity, but without finding humility. In his retirement at Gorhamsbury he sought comfort in philosophy, intellectual pursuits, and cultivating his garden. Worshipping the intellect, it was enough to know, and such knowledge did not need to proceed to action for it was sufficient of itself, 'the truth of being and the truth of knowing are one'.[19] Bacon stood at the watershed of a changing pattern of knowledge, between knowledge of the world derived from revelation, and knowledge of the world derived from observation and experiment, and he was above all others of his age the thinker who organized the new systems of knowledge which led to the scientific age. He even saw God through man, and not man through God. With cool, delicate, rhythmical prose he analysed contemporary life with its ambitions, its deviousness, its ceremonial and its worldly wisdom, and left it where it was, described as by an onlooker, but undisturbed by any thought of judgement to come. His philosophical writings give the impression of a man watching a passing show while he himself is not involved save in observation and analysis. Bacon was interested in man and in the variety of his diversions. His most telling argument for believing in God in his Essay on 'Atheism' is that 'they that deny a God destroy man's nobility; for certainly man is of kin to the beasts by his body, and if he be not kin to God by the Spirit he is a base and ignoble nature'.[20] Man was a noble creature, there had to be a God to ensure this nobility! If Bacon was not a child of the Renaissance he was certainly a foster-child. He was born in the same century as Rabelais and for his style of writing he took Montaigne, and the Essay, as his models. Like More, he had his vision of a Utopian world in the *New Atlantis*, a scientific, intellectual world, osten-

[19] Edith Sichel, *The Renaissance*, p. 213.
[20] Francis Bacon, *Essays*, 'Atheism'.

sibly Christian, but firmly rooted in a rationalism hardly elevated by Grace. If the Renaissance found in classical authors, and the Greek view of life, an assertion of man as the measure of all things, a belief in the dignity of man allied to intellectual power; a worship of nature riotous in its fecundity, voluptuous in its vitality, which lies at the heart of paganism; and above all, the 'do what you will' philosophy of life enscribed on the portal of Rabelais's Utopian cloister, then Bacon was at least a foster-child of the Renaissance. Like the Renaissance man, he had no conscience, no guiding star save his own advancement, and when he fell he made the best of it without learning the spiritual lessons of his humiliations. Puritanism was also, in some ways, a child of the Renaissance, at least of the English model, for it pleaded the virtues of holiness and discipline with words rather than heroic poverty. It produced no anchorites, no hermits, no men of the Thebaid, no flagellants, no St John's of the Cross, no hair shirts, no rigorous ascetics. What it did produce, however, was words in sermon after sermon, tract after tract, and a family discipline of prayer and meditation suitable for those who had to live in the world but were sure they were not of it. The Renaissance in England in its secular aspect differed from that in Europe, particularly the South of Europe, in that the Renaissance insight in England expressed itself in words and music rather than in painting, sculpture and architecture. No painter in the sixteenth-century England could match Raphael or Michelangelo, or any of the great Florentine painters and sculptors. Nor could the English Renaissance match the flowering of French architecture in Fontainbleau, the Louvre, the Tuilleries, or the chateaux of the Loire Valley. But what nation could match in poetry, drama, or prose, the world of Shakespeare, Marvell, Ben Johnson, Webster, Massinger, Beaumont and Fletcher, Spenser, Sidney, More, Wyatt, Raleigh, Hooker, Donne, the Cranmer of the Prayer Book, and not least the authorized version of the Scriptures, the only literary masterpiece produced by a Committee! The English Renaissance was a riot of words, words which pointed to the glory of life, of love, and of man's courage and despair, with the confident, lustful, brilliant life-affirming eyes of supposed pagan antiquity, and crowned it all with laughter, the laughter which said Rabelais belonged to man alone. In its reliance on the Word, Puritanism too was a child of the English Renaissance. Sermon-tasting was as popular as play-going, and to the education-loving, rising middle-class families, with their servants and apprentices, more exciting. But the sermons live in a different world from the plays and the poetry. It is as if two different universes exist side by side. The one draws upon Greek and European History and legend, and the other draws exclusively upon the Scriptures.

Elizabethan and Jacobean poetry have moving religious undertones, but it is the cultic religion of reformed Anglicanism which sees God through man, and not man through God, and whilst it sees God through man, it sees man himself through nature, which is his cradle, his stage, and his tomb. Religion in the dramatists and poets merely crowns man the lord of creation. 'The great poet writing himself, writes his time',[21] and the times were cynical and disillusioned if Shakespeare or Ben Jonson are any measure of them. Yet, in the disillusionment is man, the hero, noble in reason, like an angel in action, the beauty of the world, the paragon of animals, in fact, how like a god'.[22] Not that this paragon always behaved nobly; even Renaissance man recognized this, and so Machiavelli laid it down that Princes must necessarily assume that all men are bad, as they organize their State. Yet this was not the divine pessimism of the Gospel, but a defence-mechanism in the struggle for power which kept the ruler alert for any rivals. As for man himself, noble though he is, and god-like, sometimes fortune turns against him and he must suffer the whips and scorns of time, the frustrations of his efforts, the unrequited wrongs, the oppressor's hatred, the burden of a weary life. He could end it all in self-destruction but for the 'dread of something after death'. For, as Bacon also wrote, 'men fear death as children fear to go in the dark, and as that natural fear of children is increased with tales, so is the other'.[23] It is this that makes man heed 'those ills we have, than fly to others that we know not of'.[24] Renaissance man at his best was a stoic, and

[21] T. S. Eliot, *Selected Essays*, p. 137.
[22] *Hamlet*, Act 2, Scene 2.
[23] Francis Bacon, *Essays*, 'Of Death'
[24] *Hamlet*, Act 3, Scene 1.

at his worst a coward, for his image was not designed for adversity.

The Puritan, however, believed that the purpose of religion was to fit men for adversity, so that even the elect should look out for a rainy day. The difference between the way Renaissance man, the man without God, faced adversity, and the way the Saint faced it, was that the one bore his cross, while the other took it up and carried it. To the one adversity was bad luck, to the other it was an act of God. The one endured it without complaint if he could, the other accepted it as within the redeeming purpose of God.

For it was 'God only who does good or evil', said John Preston preaching before the House of Commons, 'and this to every Nation, Church and Kingdom, and even to particular persons'.[25] Consequently, whatever happens happens because God permits it or causes it. So afflictions come to the faithful not by chance but by the providence of God,[26] and must be taken up willingly and borne patiently. These afflictions are part of taking up the Cross of Christ, and so the ways of God are full of crosses,[27] for, as Calvin says: 'God arms the devil as well as the wicked, and sits as umpire, to try the patience of the Christian soul.'[28] Afflictions, crosses, trials were the lot of the Saint as of the Sinner, but the Saint was encouraged by the Puritan Preachers not merely to endure with a patience that came from the possession of the Holy Spirit, but to expect crosses, even persecution and death in obedience to Christ's command to follow Him. The afflictions of the Godly willingly borne were a sign of their adoption, and, as William Perkins says, 'the King's Highway to Heaven'.[29] In fact, 'if we find our ways full of jollity, we have cause to suspect them',[30] as if a man was going to a city and was told beforehand that the way was narrow, and full of obstacles, with many temptations to leave the path, yet found no such opposition, no such crosses or difficulties, he could be sure he was not on the

[25] John Preston, *Golden Sceptre* (Sermon to House of Commons), p. 235

[26] Ian Breward, *William Perkins*, p. 242

[27] John Preston, *The Doctrine of Self-Denial*, p. 75.

[28] John Calvin, *Institutes*, Vol. 1. (T. H. Beveridge), p. 191.

[29] William Perkins, p. 244.

[30] John Preston, *The Doctrine of Self-Denial*, p. 85.

right way. But patience in bearing the cross was not enough to the Puritan, he must cultivate courage and not miss opportunities for doing good through fear or cowardice. 'If a man would purchase heaven he must pay the full price for it',[31] and part of that price might be persecution and imprisonment. This was especially so in standing for what is just and right. It was the duty of Christ's soldiers to witness for Christ and godliness, and if man did not stand out God would call him to account for 'sinful silence as much as for corrupt speech'.[32]

In their attitude to suffering, the Puritans were not masochistic. Suffering in itself was not commendable,[33] and there was no feeling that man ought to inflict suffering upon himself such as flagellation, or wearing a hair shirt, in order to subdue the flesh, even if the ostensible motives for such acts were to be incorporate mystically in the sufferings of Christ. John Preston prepared 'A Summe of Divinity' for his pupils, and for the London Puritan Conference as a guide to orthodox doctrine, and in it he says that Christ redeemed man first by His Assumption, commonly called His Incarnation and Nativity; secondly by His Humiliation; and thirdly by His Exaltation. Christ's Humiliation was His rejection by the people, and His sufferings in His trial, condemnation, crucifixion, and death. This Humiliation was the prelude to the joy that was set before Him in His Exaltation to the throne of Heaven. His Suffering was what was done to Him by the powers of darkness of this world. It was the Cross which He bore willingly for the Salvation of mankind, assuming human sin and suffering the wrath of God in our stead. In the economy of Grace, He who was without sin, was made to sin, and in His sacrifice became both Priest and Victim. In this aspect of Christ's suffering man could not follow Him, but could only accept the proffered gift of life. Yet, in so far as Christ willingly accepted these afflictions brought about by His perfect obedience to God, He was a pattern to the Saints who were seeking the same holy obedience.[34]

It was not, however, enough for the Puritan Preacher to teach

[31] Ibid., p. 92.
[32] Ibid., p. 87.
[33] Ibid., p. 105.
[34] Richard Sibbes, *Saint's Cordialls*, p. 27.

men to suffer willingly 'the slings and arrows of outrageous fortune', even if these outrages came ultimately from the God who only does good and evil. They were not in themselves commendable, but could be made so if carried in the Spirit of Christ. They could at least be made endurable if they were conceived in some way as contributing to the redemption of the world by demonstrating man's willingness to accept good or ill fortune at the hands of God without knowing exactly how such an end could be attained. The world was a fallen world, and all men suffered in some way or another. Nor was this attitude any different from the general teaching of the Church, for man was born into trouble 'as the sparks fly upwards'. It was what man made of afflictions which determined his acceptance with God and his progress in holiness. But the tendency of the generality of men was to seek the easy way out, to accumulate wealth which would eliminate the suffering of hunger and poverty; the attainment of power and respect among his neighbours which would relieve him of much pressure from those who would control his behaviour. One could even make friends with the mammon of unrighteousness which could alleviate conditions when troubles came. These last were the ways in which, what John Preston calls the 'civil man', could come to terms with life and make it at least bearable. But neither the attitude of those who sought by worldly means to create a bastion against personal suffering, nor the spiritual passivity of those who sought a pious response to the suffering actually come upon them was satisfactory to the Puritan Preacher. What they sought for was a people who went into the battle for righteousness in the service of Christ, and even looked for suffering because of their active participation in the struggle between good and evil. That is why those who truly followed Christ must expect a 'rainy day'. There were, however, compensations for, as John Preston said: 'Christ takes notice of you if you suffer for Him, so He does if men decline the Cross, cowardice may lose you your soul.'[35] It was this urgency for action which distinguished the Puritan from his Christian neighbour and it was this pressure which was continually supplied from the pulpit. 'Because you wear Christ's livery,' says Preston, 'show whose you are, for it is often easier to do the

[35] John Preston, *Doctrine of Self-Denial*, p. 87.

inward spiritual thing than the outward act.'[36] Even if the outward righteous act brings suffering, a true Christian who has experienced the grace of forgiveness of sins knows that this takes the sting out of afflictions. For the aim of the Gospel is to incorporate a forgiven man in Christ, and then even the worst condition will be pleasant and such a man will find rest in prison, in sickness and even in death.[37] But all these consolations offered to those who carried their sufferings and afflictions in triumph as Christ their Elder Brother did, were not offered merely as consolation to endurance, but to forge confident souls determined to do what was right; to walk with God and fight for His cause. The Godly were always in a minority, and so must prepare for the worst. 'This is a time of striving, of running, of activity, it is not a time of being rewarded.'[38]

In the banquet of life offered to Renaissance man, Puritanism was indeed the death's head at the Feast; a warning against personal lasciviousness, licence, cowardice, and sloth. And this was not only a warning in respect of personal morality, but against national indifference to the Gospel at home and abroad. The danger in such a warning was lest men should sink into despair, instead of being roused to action. They must see that afflictions are merely the way that God ploughs the stiff spirit of man to mould it to His own sovereign purposes. Man's spirit must be renewed, 'for God will build on nothing in us . . . whose course is to pull down before He build up. Old things must be out of request, before all become new, and without the newness of the whole man from union into Christ no interest in the new Heavens can be hoped for, where unto no defiled thing can enter.'[39]

In the economy of Salvation which demanded the humbling of man before the mighty power of God, afflictions had their appropriate uses. They were a means whereby a man was reduced to nothing so that he could fly to Christ for comfort and be filled with the Holy Spirit. For the purpose of God was not to humble man for His own pleasure but to drive him to his

[36] Ibid., p. 100.
[37] John Preston, *Golden Sceptre* (New Creature), p. 441.
[38] Ibid., p. 19.
[39] John Preston, *Saint's Qualification*, Introduction.

Salvation. It was the Puritan conviction that man would never come to Christ until he was completely stripped of his pride, and in fear and trembling cried for mercy. 'So till we be all nothing, till there be no twig to hang by, till there be no fibre to nourish us on our own bottomes, we will never come to Christ.'[40] The Saints therefore were warned what to expect from life, for Christ had warned them, 'if they were willing to undergoe it, then he takes them, else he takes them not'.[41] The Saints were encouraged to see in suffering the wrath of God against sin which was the human cause of suffering, and to accept the cross willingly as Christ did and carry it to the glory of God. There were consolations in this approach, the Saints 'would shine like stars most needed in a dark night'[42]; the fact that they not only suffered the natural afflictions of man, but also the despising and persecution of the world demonstrated the fact they were God's own family called by His name.[43] They had to expect a greater suffering than others, more crosses to carry, more afflictions to try them because they had been chosen to challenge Satan, God's great enemy, and must expect his malice. 'It is living godly that brings persecutions, the being downright, and balking nothing, because the Devil is our own enemy and will stir up men against us, he will nibble at our heels . . . the Devil lets men alone who are but indifferent, but the Saints who are his enemies, they are sure to smart for it.'[44] But the end of their journey was sure, and they could find comfort in the fact that 'God had rejoicing days for His people, as well as mourning days, faire weather as well as foule, and all to help them forward on their way to Heaven'.[45] Indeed, it is expedient that 'God depart from the Saints in outward things, for until He leave us in these, the comforts of the Holy Ghost come not so purely to us'.[46]

So, whilst the Saints were encouraged to see the skull beneath the skin of life, and to testify to this death-in-life, they were also

[40] Ibid., p. 219.
[41] John Preston, *Doctrine of Self-Denial* (1632), p. 108.
[42] Ibid., p. 91.
[43] Richard Sibbes, *Saint's Cordialls*, p. 218.
[44] John Preston, *Doctrine of Self-Denial*, p. 215.
[45] Richard Sibbes, *Saint's Cordialls*, p. 219.
[46] John Preston, *An Antidote Against Heart Fears* (1658), p. 341.

warned to see this first in themselves. They would find light and life in Christ while they were marching to Heaven, but they still had to prepare for 'a rainy day', in the knowledge that these 'cloudings do but obscure their graces not extinguish them', as the darkness of night could not extinguish the light of the stars, but merely conceal it.[47]

[47] John Preston, *An Elegant and Lively Description of Life and Death* (1632), p. 26.

SEVEN

The Godly Brotherhood

THE use of the terms 'brother' and 'brotherhood' in the history of the Church almost invariably carries monkish connotations, as if this call to fraternity needed a special context in which to be effective. The formation of a brotherhood is not, of course, an end in itself, it is always an association for some purpose, and it is the purpose which gives cohesion and form to the association. The purposes for which a brotherhood is formed can be chosen from any of a whole gamut of human aspiration, social, political, military, educational, or even the mere enjoyment of the company of others, but the dynamic of brotherhood is the adoption of some purpose. Consequently, the use of the term 'brother' or 'brotherhood' is never vague or allusive, but identifiable and concrete. This is especially true in the Christian context, where every Christian is bound to see a brother in every other Christian. As Jesus said to His disciples, 'One is your teacher and all ye are brethren'.[1]

The concept of brotherhood on the other hand is not to be confused with the concept of neighbourliness, though, of course, a brother is a neighbour by sheer contiguity. 'To love thy neighbour as thyself' is the duty and privilege of all men and is implied in their common humanity. He who proved neighbour to him who fell among thieves was he who had mercy on him, even though there was no brotherly relation between them, and it applied equally well to the Jew as to the Samaritan. The concept of a Christian brotherhood however is not primarily orientated to the service of humanity, but to communion with God and to the service of humanity for Christ's sake. The love of Christ is the dynamic of brotherhood as the blessed St Anthony said to

[1] St Matthew 23:8.

the ungrateful cripple who had turned against the monk Eulogius who nursed him, 'Do you not know it is Christ who is serving you? Was it not for Christ's sake he made himself a slave to minister to you? How dare you utter such words against Christ'. It is Christ who creates brotherhood for the Christian, setting before him the goal of perfection in a life of faith and good works.[2]

When St Paul, for example, sent the slave Onesimus back to his Christian master, Philemon, he did not demand that Philemon give him his freedom, but entreated him to see Onesimus no longer as a servant, but as a brother beloved, because Onesimus had become a Christian, and so accepted the purposes which informed the brotherhood of Christians. Brotherhood in the New Testament is always used of the brotherhood of the Saints, who have an obligation to fulfil the royal law of neighbourliness as all other men had, but whose spiritual growth in communion with God was their first concern. Brotherhood in the biblical sense is not a natural relationship, as sonship in relation to God is not a natural right. Men become sons of God by adoption into the Christian family, and their sonship is the consequence of God's gift of the Holy Spirit to them that are in Christ. Brotherhood is also a spiritual relationship existing amongst those seeking sanctification, 'for both he that sanctifieth and they that are sanctified are all one, for which cause he is not ashamed to call them brethren.[3]

The idea of Christian brotherhood is therefore intimately connected with the attainment of sanctity. In the early years of the Church this connection between the concept of brotherhood and the attainment of sanctity was applied indiscriminately to the whole Church. All Christians were brethren because they were spiritually different from the world. They were the Saints, οἱ ἁγίοι, the holy ones, and what constituted them brethren, was this common concern for sanctity. During the first three centuries of the Church's history until the Edict of Milan in AD 313, periodic persecution contained the Church, as it were, and preserved the feeling of the brotherhood of all Christians. Dionysius of Corinth writing to Soter, Bishop of Rome, around

[2] *The Lausiac History of Palladius* (SPCK) (1918), p. 95.
[3] Hebrews, 2:11–18.

170 AD, commends the great charity of the Church in Rome, 'For you have from the beginning this custom of doing good in diverse ways to all the brethren, and sending supplies to many churches in all the cities, in one place refreshing the poverty of those in need, in another helping brethren in the mines, . . . helping the Saints with abundant supply from time to time.'[4] Persecution preserved the feeling of fellowship and the consciousness of the sanctity of the whole Church.

On the other hand, the discipline of the Church on which the idea of brotherhood is founded, suffered numerous setbacks during these centuries. One aspect of this was the treatment of the 'lapsed', those who had apostasized during the persecutions and afterwards sought restitution. In these cases should the primitive severity of discipline be upheld or was there room in a growing community for indulgence to the penitent? Carthage and Rome became the centres of controversy on the question of how to treat penitent apostates. There were those in the Church who wanted to maintain a pure, spiritual Church and to exclude those who had denied the Saviour under persecution. The Novatian schism in Rome is an illustration of this attitude and the followers of the schismatic Bishop Novatian were known as the 'Cathari' or puritans. They were orthodox in faith and their stand was purely on disciplinary grounds. The growing popularity of the Church, which was gradually becoming a cultic as opposed to a sectarian organism, tended to leniency especially as some of those under sentence of death interceded for their weaker brethren. In fact, it became a kind of privilege for the 'confessors' to intercede with the Bishop for those who were penitent but cut off from Church Communion.

The controversy on how to treat the 'lapsed' in the persecution became enlarged to include the whole question of how to treat penitent sinners, adulterers, thieves, murderers and so on. Should they be restored to Church Communion if penitent? When Callistus, Bishop of Rome (219–25), absolved penitent adulterers and fornicators and restored them to Church Communion he shocked many, and was accused of lowering the whole tone of

[4] H. M. Gwatkin, *Selections from Early Christian Writers* (1897), p. 61.

the Church.[5] Not the least to be shocked was the greatest of the Latin writers of the Church, Tertullian (160–245), whose powerful satirical writings thundered against heretics, persecutors, and particularly those Christians who failed to live up to his own uncompromising view of Christian loyalty and discipline. In middle life he deliberately identified himself with the earliest of puritan sects, the Montanists, in revolt against what to him was the increasing laxness of the Church. As the Church increased in numbers it was inevitable that the problem of how to reconcile the sanctity of the whole, with the lack of sanctity in the lives of individual members, was bound to arise. The pressure to include the whole of mankind, as it were, within the Church, and to find some formula which would sustain this inclusion, led to the externalization of the structure of the Church, so that the formal acts and models of worship were defined as independent of the character of the instrument. No doubt the process was in the providence of God, but it did mean that the method of treating penitent sinners had to be modified. No longer were the 'lapsed' to be permanently excluded; there was, through confession and penitence, a means of restitution to the Communion of the Church. The Donatist controversy, upon which St Augustine wrote with such finality, exposed in what was often a vicious dialogue, the guide-lines upon which the Church was to move. The Church for the foreseeable future was not seen as an organism which appeared or disappeared with the sanctity of the members. She was the divine society which begins with the love of God and leads to Heaven, as opposed to the worldly kingdom which begins in the love of self and ends in Hell.[6] But this movement of definition argued by some of the greatest thinkers of that or any age, tended inevitably to undervalue sanctity as a possibility of present possession, which seems to be implied in the New Testament. Yet, the words of our Lord, 'Be ye perfect, as your heavenly Father is perfect' still stood as a challenge to the Christian man, and there were those who accepted the challenge in reliance on the promises of the Holy Spirit. These were the monks, hermits, and anchorites whose austerity, discipline and devotion to God still haunt a fragmented Church and a

[5] Edwyn Bevan, *Christianity* (1932), ch. 5, p. 78.
[6] St Augustine, *The City of God* (John Grant, 1909), Bk. 14, ch. 28.

demoralized philosophy of life. Whether the monastic movement is viewed as a reaction to the enervating influence of a cultic Church, or as the charismatic necessity for primary groups which sweeten and leaven the whole mixture of a Christian presence, or, as the self-centred concern for personal salvation, the concept of sanctity and its correlative 'brotherhood' assumed a new consciousness in the economy of salvation. It was in the Egyptian desert that a conscious movement began to seek for and attain a present sanctity in the dedicated asceticism of hermits and monks.

Bishop Palladius, the John Aubrey of the Desert Monks, records with artless sympathy the stories of the anchorites and ascetics of the Egyptian desert in their struggles to attain ἀπαθεία or detachment from the world. These were the first monastic communities which in their development in the early part of the fourth century sought to make explicit what was implied in the teaching of apostolic Christianity. Christians were bound to renounce the aspirations and the satisfactions of the world, and so, from the first, asceticism was inherent in the Christian Gospel.

Even the simple Apostolic commandment to the first Christians to abstain from idolatry which has no relevance to Western Christianity today, must have had a traumatic effect in an age where every social act, even the buying of meat, was associated with some aspect of pagan worship. No doubt as the Church grew in numbers there was much compromise, and some, such as Demas, forsook the Church 'having loved this present age'. But there were those who lived ascetic lives at home, bearing 'the whole yoke of the Lord'.[7] In the world, but not of it. This dichotomy in life produced for the Christian ascetic a style of living, a pattern of behaviour, which became a model as it were for the life of renunciation. It was a life of self-discipline, a mortifying of the flesh, a refusal to surrender to the senses, undergirded by prayer and meditation. Prayer was as important as renunciation in the life of faith, for the ascetic objective was not renunciation or detachment for its own sake, but as a means of drawing closer in spirit to God and the Saviour in whom was the fount of perfection.

Why Christian monasticism originated in the Egyptian Desert

[7] *Didache*, ch. 6.

is a matter for conjecture. Egypt was not as strong a centre of Christianity as Asia Minor where St. Paul and his companions founded the first Christian churches outside Jerusalem, but Egypt had produced, certainly in Alexandria, a significant church with a great teaching tradition not averse to experiments in theological and philosophical thinking through the work of Clement of Alexandria, and Origen. There was also an ascetic tradition there, enough to cause the young Origen to mutilate himself so as to subdue the lusts of the flesh! This intemperate interpretation of Matthew 19:12 showed a zeal for sanctity more Asiatic than Roman and diminished the influence of one who was otherwise a great and original thinker. Self-mutilation, even to achieve detachment, could not really appeal to those who inherited the mantle of the Caesars. Prudence, industry, temperance, and fortitude were the virtues of Rome, and Christian Rome could never forget them, even though they superimposed faith, hope and charity as evangelical objectives. In the Holy Roman Empire the manly virtues of Augustan Rome were gathered together, as it were, in the virtues of discipline and obedience. The Alexandrian School of theology inheriting and baptizing into the Faith elements of the philosophy of Porphyry and Plotinus, had its grass roots in Plato and the Hellenistic world. The attainment of ἀπάθεια was a Greek concept and one beloved of the stoic philosophers. But whereas the Greeks sought to attain detachment by practising all things in moderation, the 'mean' of life, sustained by the satisfactions of philosophy, the desert hermits and the anchorites filled the concept with Scriptural content, the mortification of the flesh, so prominent in Pauline thinking as the way, not to 'know thyself', but to be filled with the Spirit of Christ. The purging of the flesh was the first step to holiness.

Tradition has it that the infiltration of the Egyptian Desert by the anchorites and hermits which occurred in the third and fourth century AD had its origin in the Decian persecution (AD 250). Both Eusebius and Jerome say that this was the historic occasion of the movement.[8] The Church had grown considerably through the peaceful first half of the third century. The Church of Rome in AD 251, for instance, had forty-six

[8] Eusebius, *History of the Church VI*, p. 42 and Jerome, *Vita Pauli.*

priests and seven deacons, besides 150 others in minor orders. It also supported about 1,500 widows and orphans out of its charity. The Church however was still not a '*religio licita*', but it was prosperous, living in a half world of approval, though still subject to setbacks of local violence, and the personal attitudes of the Emperors, which sometimes issued in persecution. During the Decian persecution hundreds of anchorites fled from the cities of Egypt into the Desert and remained there after the persecutions ceased. They had found an ideal place for their austerities. The Desert was at least warm, with water from the Nile near at hand. It was within reach of the populous Egyptian cities and not too far from those of Asia Minor. This encouraged hordes of sightseers who carried the hermits' fame all over the Roman Empire. There was an air of gamesmanship about the whole movement, 'the athletes of Christ'[9] as the hermits were called, struggling to subdue the flesh in the 'arena of piety',[10] in the desert. During the first three centuries of the Christian Church the heroes of the Church were the martyrs who remained steadfast even unto death in the persecutions. After the reign of Constantine, who declared Christianity a '*religio licita*', martyrdom ceased. It was the monks of the desert who took their place in Christian romanticism, fighting the good fight against the demonic forces of evil which sought to debase man by enslaving him to his lower nature. The desert was the place for these heroes, for everyone knew that the desert was the homeland of demons, evil spirits having a special fondness for waterless places! Christ's athletes went to challenge them on their own ground. Their weapons were prayer and meditation on the Holy Scriptures which were often learned by heart,[11] frequent communion, and the continued use of the Agape,[12] at which one brother or another was responsible for providing the food. In this way they were not only seeking perfection but thought of themselves as 'guarding' the walls of the Church.[13] But their special spiritual distinction was the mortification of the flesh to

[9] *The Lausiac History of Palladius*, p. 79.
[10] Ibid., pp. 36 and 104.
[11] Ibid., p. 116.
[12] Ibid., p. 72.
[13] Ibid., p. 86.

conquer lust and gluttony in particular. These are the temptations most often mentioned and which were the most prominent sins of an Empire in decline. It is not to be thought that the thousands of men and women who fled to the desert over two centuries necessarily went there just to practise perfection. Some, undoubtedly, went for religious motives, others went to escape the intolerable burden of taxation which was especially onerous in Egypt, the granary of Rome, due to the tightening hold of the central government. The populace of Rome had to be fed. Bread and circuses was the diet of the people who had to be pleasured and amused at the expense of the Empire. The temptation to escape by running away was very strong. A similar process can be discerned in the migration of Puritans to the New World in the seventeenth century, partly religious and partly economic. But whatever the reasons, the migration of thousands into the Egyptian Desert gave a new impetus to the concept of Christian self-discipline to the Church and kept alive the mystique of Sainthood which found its dynamic in monasticism during the Middle Ages and in Puritanism in Reformation England. St Anthony organized these desert saints at the turn of the fourth century. Great colonies of monks arose in the north of the desert, inland from Alexandria. Their cells were grouped around a central church or house of prayer where the monks met for worship on Saturdays and Sundays. But, essentially each monk made his own rule and exercised his own discipline. When Palladius visited this area there were about 7,000 monks who earned their own living by linen-manufacture, or worked in the bakeries, or kitchens, or cultivated such garden plots as they were able to make. There were doctors and confectioners, and even wine was on sale. Eight priests served the church only on Saturday and Sunday, but at certain hours each monk recited or sang the psalms.[14] Many miles to the south of Alexandria, in the Thebaid, Palladius visited a different kind of monastic community founded by Pachomius (*c.* AD 315) namely, communities of monks who lived a communal life under a common rule with a Superior as the main principle. These constituted an order such as developed in the West, where, despite the deprivation to monastic life brought about by the barbarian invasions, a similar form of disciplined

[14] *The Lausiac History of Palladius,* Ch. VII.

asceticism was revived by St Benedict in the sixth century AD. It was the Rule of St Benedict, endorsed by Pope Gregory, which determined the form which monastic asceticism assumed in the Middle Ages throughout the whole of Catholic Christendom.

But, whatever the monks of the desert were, coenobitic, or eremitic, they were part of a brotherhood who were making the 'journey of the Spirit'[15], sharing a conviction that perfection was to be found through prayer and self-discipline, while engaging in good activities the 'mother of spiritual self-culture'.[16] Palladius himself was a monk, and in the prologue to his book written for the spiritual consolation of Lausus, Chamberlain of the Court of Theodosius II, he mentions that he wrote his book when he was fifty-six years of age, in the twentieth year of his episcopate, and his thirty-third year in the Society of the Brethren.[17] He had long left his monastery travelling to Jerusalem, to Egypt, and back to Jerusalem and was consecrated Bishop of Helenapolis in about AD 400, but he still thought of himself as belonging to the Society of the monastic brethren. As, indeed, did St Anselm, centuries later, from the throne of Canterbury long to renew his fellowship with the 'brethren' in the Monastery at Bec; 'in heart belonging to them after God'.[18] St Augustine mentions in his *Confessions* that though he had lived in Milan a long time he had not heard until he came to Rome of a monastery outside the walls of Milan 'full of good brethren'.[19] St Benedict in the Rule he framed for his monks in the sixth century constantly refers to them as 'the brethren', and it was in this tradition that St Francis seven centuries later called his Order by the title of the Fratres Minores or the lesser brethren. Throughout the Middle Ages whenever the words 'brethren' or 'brotherhood' are mentioned in a religious context, they almost invariably refer to monks or friars, in other words, to groups of men (women were referred to as sisters) who pursued the objectives of saintliness in preaching conversion, and practising godliness. On the eve of the Reformation there were,

[15] Ibid., p. 139.
[16] Ibid., p. 42.
[17] Ibid., p. 40.
[18] St Anselm, *Cur Deus Homo* (The Ancient and Modern Library of Theological Lit.), p. 136.
[19] St Augustine. *Confessions*, Ibid., p. 144.

therefore, within the context of Church-life, groups dedicated to the attainment of sanctity, forming subsidiary brotherhoods, pursuing under various disciplines a perfection which was the demonstration of divine election in all its fullness. It is not important here, whether these objectives were well pursued or not, what is important is that the Church recognized the presence and relevance of such brotherhoods. In those lands where the Reformation triumphed these brotherhoods were all eliminated within the space of two or three decades, possibly with justification, but this drastic surgery did not eliminate the human desire for closer fellowships in the religious life, and a more disciplined effort for personal holiness. The fact was that the dynamic which produced the effort to achieve sanctity in 'brotherhoods' had declined in the two centuries before the Reformation, and monasticism itself had become integrated into the hierarchical structure of the Church, and shared its laxity and corruption. This process had gone on throughout the later Middle Ages, so that monasticism had virtually become an arm of the Papacy to be used at will to sustain the authority of the Pope. With the dissolution of the monasteries came the dissolution of derivative brotherhoods and sodalities, such as those dedicated to particular altars of parish churches, and religion in England at least was stripped of its variety, as of much of its property, while worship was eventually forced into narrow conformist exercises, centring mainly in the two services of Morning and Evening Prayer, with such sacraments and rites as the Book of Common Prayer appointed.[20] What the establishment of religion in Reformation England did not provide for was what Dr H. B. Workman calls a 'safety valve for the energy of the Church',[21] such as was supplied by monasticism during the Middle Ages. This energy can be defined under the broad headings of a concern for the salvation of souls by conversion and the desire for holiness. St Ambrose describes the Church of his day as making provision for the 'soaring of eagles' as well as for the 'fluttering of sparrows'.[22] The Elizabethan settlement pro-

[20] Charles Wheatley, *Book of Common Prayer* (1858), p. 378.
[21] H. B. Workman, *The Evolution of the Monastic Ideal*, p.333.
[22] Ibid., p. 334.

vided elegantly for the 'fluttering of sparrows', but neglected the 'soaring of eagles'.

The Puritan Movement is to the Elizabethan Church what monasticism was to the Medieval Church. It expressed Gospel energy always unsatisfied with the lowest common denominator syndrome of Reformed religion, and in its desire for evangelical preaching and concern for disciplined and holy lives it formed brotherhoods of preachers dedicated for the pursuit of those ends. Thus the name 'brother' became a distinguishing mark of the Puritan in the century of its rise and disintegration into sectarian churches. The term 'brother' or 'brethren' was a term which the godly preachers and their lay supporters appropriated to themselves as Richard Bancroft discerned when he collected evidence to prosecute the Preachers in the Star Chamber. His purpose was to demonstrate that Puritanism was a conspiracy to overthrow the hierarchical structure of the Church, and then Queen Elizabeth's government. However, he tried to prove too much, and his charge against the Preachers of seditious conduct was unproven. However, he did put his finger on the fact that these Preachers had formed themselves into a Brotherhood within the orbit of the National Church.[23] Bancroft's error was to misunderstand the purpose for which the Preachers formed a 'brotherhood'. The brotherhood was that of evangelical preachers who sought to convert men from an unholy life to a life of godliness with its attendant discipline. This was the true character of a Puritan and it embraced not only the godly preachers, but godly laymen as well. This soubriquet of 'brotherhood' was used by the opponents of Puritanism to describe them in much the same way as the word 'comrade' today denotes a communist or someone on the left of the political scene, or the word 'methodist' in the eighteenth century denoted a follower of the Wesleys. Ben Jonson's odious Puritan, Zeal-of-the-Land Busy in *Bartholomew Fair* is called 'Brother Busy', or a 'Brother of Banbury', Banbury being one of the most forceful centres of Puritanism. All the clichés of the Godly Preachers are caricatured in his speeches. Brother Busy is moved by the spirit; he prophesies; everything at the Fair is vanity; when he is put in the stocks he rejoices in

[23] R. Bancroft, *Dangerous Positions*, pp. 120 and 122, also G. Downame, *Two Sermons*, p. 5.

his affliction 'for it is his calling to "suffer" there'; even the puppets are condemned because the men dress as women and the women as men. The play was first performed for King James and was meant to denigrate the 'brethren' or the 'faction' as the Prologue addressed to the King shows. It also assumed the King's approval of the fun poked at the Puritans 'whereof the petulant ways, yourself have known and have been vexed with long'.[24] *Bartholomew Fair* was written and presented at Court in 1614 and represents the level to which the fortunes of the Godly Preachers had fallen, to be so publicly, and with royal approval, caricatured. It would have been impossible to present such a play in the Court of Queen Elizabeth. Not that she might have objected, but the powerful patrons of the godly brethren would have rendered such an effort impossible. Leicester, Walsingham, even Burleigh had more than sympathy with the Preachers, so indeed did Sir Fulke Greville, later Lord Brooke, who was one of the Queen's favourites. James however disliked Puritans, although he loved preaching, and was always pleased in his indecisive way to see them taken down a peg or two. There were powerful men in the Court such as the Earl of Pembroke, and Sir Fulke Greville, who became Chancellor of the Exchequer in 1614, who had some sympathy for them. But none of these men were the King's Favourite in the way that Robert Carr was, and it was Carr's promoters, the Catholic Howard group at Court whose influence was the most powerful during the first decade of James's reign. But 1614 was to prove a turning point for the Puritan brethren. It was in that year that James visited Cambridge, and John Preston by a lucky accident was brought to his notice and approval, at which Sir Fulke Greville attached him to his person by giving him a pension of £50 per annum. It was also about that time that James met the young George Villiers with considerable consequences for the Puritan movement, which, under Villiers's patronage, became acceptable at Court.

The Puritan Brotherhood, whose meetings, known as 'prophesyings', had been suppressed by Elizabeth, began again to take on a public and open form, while the laity in the Commons and Lords became more openly associated with them. John Preston

[24] Ben Jonson, *Bartholomew Fair*, prologue to the King's Majesty.

had first been called a Puritan when as a young don at Queens' he had refused to allow one of his pupils to appear in a play dressed as a woman. From this he graduated to the Puritan element in the Church and soon came to lead them. And, although offered high office in the hierarchy of the Church and State, he steadily refused to compromise the sense of equality among the Godly preachers which is denoted by the word 'brother' or 'brethren'. He remained throughout his ministry one of the godly brotherhood of Preachers and only accepted appointments which extended the opportunity for godly preaching. This sense of brotherhood among the Godly Preachers and their lay supporters was a very real spiritual support to the Puritan movement. The term identified a stratum of people who found their spiritual inspiration in preaching and sermons; the pursuit of a godly disciplined life, in prayer, supported by Bible-study and Sabbath observance; their spiritual home among the Saints who were marching to Zion; and the 'church', the community of the elect chosen by the Holy Spirit and subject only to Christ and to no earthly sovereignty. The substance of this spiritual characterization remains more or less constant throughout the history of the Puritan movement, despite the greater or lesser emphasis placed by small groups on one aspect or another.

Paul S. Seaver has emphasized in his study of the Puritan Lectureships the importance of the lay support the Preachers received, a support which gave the laity of a parish or town corporation, a control over the appointment of the Preachers since they paid his salary. But much more was expected of the laity than material support for the preaching Brotherhood; they were expected to identify themselves personally with the godly aims which were the substance of the preaching. The 'prophesyings' in Elizabethan times were not only intended to test the calling and gifts of ministers before admitting them into the brotherhood of Preachers,[25] but to involve the laity in the godly life. Consequently, the word 'brother' first adopted by the Preachers to describe their company, came to be applied to the laity who followed them. When Wentworth, writing to Laud,

[25] Irvonwy Morgan, *The Godly Preachers of the Elizabethan Church*, ch. 3.

describes John Hampden as a 'great brother',[26] he identifies him as a Puritan. The same criteria ought also to be applied to Sir John Eliot, a personal friend of John Hampden, despite the fact that S. R. Gardiner,[27] John Forster,[28] and H. R. Williamson,[29] in their studies of the period say he was not a Puritan. Unlike Chief Justice Yelverton, who, when trying the case of Peter Smart, a canon of Durham, said that 'he had always been accounted a Puritan and thanked God for it',[30] Eliot never expressly claimed to be a Puritan. However, if a man is judged by the company he keeps then Eliot certainly looked like one. He was intimately associated with the Puritan group of the Earl of Warwick, Lord Saye, Strode and Rich, who, with John Preston were advising the Duke of Buckingham when he returned from Spain in 1623, after the failure of the Spanish marriage negotiations.[31] Eliot's view of the relationship between the Church and State was Puritan rather than the Erastian Protestantism of the Arminian divines, for he believed that the Church and Commonwealth were two distinct States, and that the Church had a right to ex-communicate monarchs.[32] When he was allowed out of the Marshalsea Prison in 1629 to go to church, it was to the 'lectures' at St Mary Overies he went and St Mary Overies at that time was organized as a 'Puritan' Church with 'Lecturers' rather than incumbents. His daughter, Elizabeth, married Lord Saye's son, Nathaniel, and the young Earl of Lincoln, a strong Puritan, was a friend of his, and was one of the few who braved the wrath of the King and visited him in the Tower just before he died. Eliot of course has been singled out as being one of the great Parliamentary defenders of the liberty of Englishmen, on a par with John Pym and John Hampden, and all his attitudes breathe Jacobean Puritanism, not least in his dedicated opposition to tyranny whether of Church or State. Unlike many writers on Sir John Eliot, who do not discuss his religion, H. R.

[26] Strafford's *Letters and Dispatches*, Wentworth to Laud, Nov. 27, 1637.

[27] S. R. Gardiner, *History of England*, Vol. 5, p. 343.

[28] John Forster, *Sir John Eliot*, Vol. 1, p. 10.

[29] H. R. Williamson, *Four Stuart Portraits*, p. 86.

[30] Bp Cousins, *Correspondence* (Surtees Society), Vol. 1. Introduction.

[31] John Hacket, *Life of Archbishop Williams*, part 2, p. 18.

[32] John Eliot, *De Jure Majestatis*, pp. 136 and 137.

Williamson does, and comes to the conclusion that his religion was a kind of 'classical theism' which he deduces from an exercise that Eliot wrote in prison to while away the time, called *The Monarchie of Man.* Eliot certainly had a great admiration for classical writers, but this was never a substitute for Christianity in his mind. Indeed, he saw that some of his friends would misunderstand his treatise, because of his pre-occupation with the work of classical authors, rather than Biblical and Christian history, and he wrote a preface to explain that his treatise was a political essay and not a religious tract.[33] Such evidence as we have of his religion is to be found in his letters written from the Tower, and particularly those written to that impeccable Puritan, Sir Richard Knightley, to whose home John Preston went to die. In twelve of the fourteen extant letters written by John Eliot, to the Puritan Squire, he signs himself by some such phrase as 'your friend and Brother', and it is impossible to suppose that Eliot did not understand the significance of the term 'Brother' in the context of the time.

The concept of a 'Brotherhood' which included both clergy and laity and which features so prominently in Puritan writings was not a nickname given to men by their adversaries, but a name the Preachers and their lay supporters adopted themselves. They met in brotherhoods under a rule to develop and practise holy living. To this end they drew their inspirations not only from sermons and conferences but also from manuals of behaviour described as 'guides to godliness', which poured forth from the Preachers for the guidance of those who could be drawn from a 'general support of Christianity to a daily and particular care of godliness'.[34] Most of these guides to godliness were series of sermons gathered together and printed, and were issued again and again in the first half of the seventeenth century.[35] The Preacher asserted that faith was not enough by itself, only faith and a godly life could bring a man to heaven, and this godly life, the achievement of sanctity, had to be practised by 'flying evil

33 John Forster, *Sir John Eliot*, Vol. 2, p. 161.

34 Richard Rogers, *Seven Treatises*, p. 593.

35 Irvonwy Morgan, *The Godly Preachers of the Elizabethan Church*, ch. 4.

and doing good' under a strict personal and ecclesiastical discipline.

It was this concern for godly discipline that made John Foxe characterize the Puritans as 'new monks', while Richard Rogers, the Preacher of Weathersfield, who was one of the earliest of the Puritan Preachers, defended a disciplined godliness as being 'no monkerie'. But there was an affinity with the aims of monachism, and the guides to godliness were written to demonstrate that the claims of the Papists, that they only were concerned with godliness, were false. The concept of a brotherhood dedicated to the attainment of sanctity demanded a disciplined obedience, in which the discipline of personal obedience in the individual was re-inforced by the discipline of the group. The problem of the Godly Preachers therefore was how to structure this discipline. They began by the creation of preaching Brotherhoods in a purely charismatic fashion such as is described in the Minutes of the Dedham Brotherhood. This movement blossomed into the 'Prophesyings' of the time of Elizabeth I, which were suppressed by the Queen despite the encouragement given to the movement by Archbishop Grindal. One aspect of the movement sought to bring a 'presbyterian' reform of discipline into the English Church, but this again was suppressed by Archbishop Bancroft, and the Godly Preachers were left to preach on conversion and sanctity where they could find an audience who were prepared to engage them as 'Lecturers' in parish or borough. But the concept of brotherhood was still kept alive by the Preachers, and given some public form in the 'conferences' and 'fasts' which they encouraged. One place where a godly discipline could be encouraged and supported was the family unit. The family was a natural unit in society with its own structure of discipline from the father, to the wife, to the children, the servants and the workmen in workshop or estate, and the Preachers vigorously encouraged the godly discipline of piety and holiness in every family they could influence.

The Church, however, was a different matter, for every soul born into a Christian State was a member of the Church, and the Puritans believed unequivocably in a national church. They were the hammer of schismatics until they too were hammered by Archbishop Laud. To the Preachers of the Jacobean age an outward profession of religion was a built-in constituent of a Christian presence,[36] for errors in opinion were worse than errors in practice,[37] and 'it was a monstrous thing that men should be openly profane'.[38] In fact, it was necessary to restrain men whose 'wills were set on hurtful things',[39] for a law was weakened where it was not cared for.[40] This insistence that the whole community of a parish should respect the obligation of church attendance even when some secretly, or even openly, offended against Christian moral standards, led to a charge of hypocrisy in those who professed a holiness they could not always practice. The retort of the Preachers was that the real hypocrites were not those who were trying to be holy, but those who were content not to try; those who were satisfied with merely formal worship and who just did what was formally required of them by their faith. The hypocrite to the Puritan was merely the Civil Man.[41] Consequently, hypocrisy was not the eighth deadly sin that it has become for the twentieth century. It was merely the state of the natural man. In some ways there was even a kind of merit in hypocrisy, since hypocrisy was, to quote the aphorism of La Rochefoucauld, 'the homage that vice pays to virtue'.[42] It was this homage to virtue that primarily mattered since without this approval there could be no conversion, no godliness, no journey to heaven. The sad thing about hypocrisy to the Preacher was that it 'brings forth no endeavours';[43] and the burden of the Preacher was therefore that all men must make the effort to 'live godly' as God demanded. That was why God loved adverbs better than verbs;[44] effective faith, diligent hope, fruitful love, were the qualifications that godliness demanded in the evangelical virtues, and these saving graces could only be produced in the fellowship of the Saints. Indeed, a man could not even

[36] John Preston, *The Golden Sceptre* (1639), p. 62.
[37] John Preston, *The Breastplate of Faith and Love*, p. 212.
[38] John Preston, *An Elegant and Lively Description* (1932), p. 45.
[39] John Preston, *The Golden Sceptre* (The Church's Marriage), p. 32.
[40] Ibid., (Omission of Duties), p. 252.
[41] John Preston, *An Elegant and Lively Description*, p. 107.
[42] La Rochefoucauld, *Les Maxims*, p. 218.
[43] John Preston, *The New Covenant*, p. 35.
[44] John Preston, *The Doctrine of Self-Denial* (1632), p. 93.

love the Lord unless he first learn to 'love the Brethren'.[45] And, while a hypocrite could do much, as John Preston says,[46] he could only do more if he identified himself with 'the Brethren'. To love the society of 'the Brethren' who were seeking godliness by the practice of faith and good works, was the first step to sanctity.

[45] John Preston, *The Saint's Qualification* (1637), (A Heavenly Treatise), pp. 30, 31.

[46] John Preston, *An Elegant and Lively Description*, p. 67.

EIGHT

When the Saints go Marching In

THAT John Preston could think of the Duke of Buckingham as one of the 'Saints' appears unlikely only if one accepts the popular image of the narrow, bigoted, priggish, joyless Puritan of Ben Jonson's or Macaulay's caricatures, who would have been like a fish out of water at Court. But Preston, Puritan though he was, was a courtier, spohisticated, cultured, and intelligent, and would have been quite as at home in the Sun King's Court in France, as he was in that of James I. His enemies likened him to Aqua Viva, the general of the Jesuits,[1] and he does give the impression of moving behind the scenes in pressing the purposes of Puritanism; a Puritan, '*Eminence Grise*' as it were! Archbishop Laud recognized, as did others, that there was a resemblance between the Puritan and the Jesuit, and says it was because they both believed that 'the sermons and preaching by word of mouth of the lawfully sent pastors and doctors of the Church are able to create in us divine and infallible faith; they are the very Word of God'.[2]

The Puritan and the Jesuit both knew the answers, as it were, though their answers were different. It was this certainty, this assurance, which annoyed and irritated Laud and the humanist Arminian divines. It was this kind of assurance that Bishop Neill meant when he heard Preston preach at Court in 1627, and sourly remarked that Preston spoke 'as if he were familiar with God'. Yet, this is what 'Sainthood' meant to the Puritan, 'to be familiar with God';[3] with God the all-sufficient, who was Judge, Saviour, and Father of His chosen people; who comforted them

[1] Irvonwy Morgan, *Prince Charles's Puritan Chaplain*, p. 47.
[2] Ibid., p. 39.
[3] John Preston, *Saint's Qualification* (Saint's Spiritual Strength), p. 100.

with the riches of mercy, yet chastised them with the rod of His anger, who demanded their complete submission but offered them the glory of His friendship on earth, and the splendour of His heaven after death; who dragged them by His elective grace through the 'Slough of Despond'; pushed them up Hill Difficulty; chained the lions in their path; warned against Giant Despair; pleaded with them in Doubting Castle; guided them through Vanity Fair; enabled them to escape Giant Pope; struggled with them in the Valley of Humiliation; brought them to Jordan River in sight of the Land of Canaan; and blew the trumpets of Victory for them 'on the other side'. The Puritan was the eternal pilgrim travelling to the promised land; the eternal warrior fighting the fiery darts of the Devil and all his angels for the honour of God and the love of His Saints. Buckingham did not quite measure up to this perhaps, but Preston thought that he might if he trusted his Puritan allies in Parliament, rejected the overtures of the Arminian divines, and helped the Kingdom of Grace abroad in supporting the Elector Palatine.

Yet, despite this political interest, Puritanism was essentially an attempt to spiritualize religion in conversion and godly living. Those to whom the grace of conversion and the call to holiness were given, were the elect of God, and, if there were things in the movement, social changes and benefits, which, to use the words of Christopher Hill, might 'appeal to laymen',[4] they were in the nature of uncovenanted mercies, side effects as it were.

The Jacobean age was peculiarly the time when Puritanism was able to examine and persuade spiritual religion under the auspices of the Godly Preachers. In Elizabethan times the movement was bedevilled by a Church-structure controversy—as between the merits of Episcopacy or Presbyterianism—a controversy exhaustively and splendidly examined by Patrick Collinson in his *The Elizabethan Puritan Movement*. After 1640 the movement exhausted itself in political controversy, centred in Parliament, a controversy which was only kept in bounds by the imposition of a 'Godless rule'[5] by Cromwell. That is a rule

[4] Christopher Hill, *Society and Puritanism*, p. 39.
[5] William Lamont, *Godly Rule*, Ch. 6.

which within bounds allowed any form of Christian commitment, provided that moral issues were publicly agreed.

Jacobean religion therefore was nicely poised between the Arminian and Calvinist interpretation of the Faith, neither of which was in the ascendant. The Church-structure controversy had died down; there were no really radical Puritan proposals introduced into Parliamentary debates and people flocked to hear the Godly Preachers, who fought the spiritual welfare in sermon after sermon, travelled the pilgrim road in lecture after lecture, and analysed sin and holiness with an expertise never equalled before or since. It was evangelical preaching on a Calvinist basis expounded with passion and pleading. It was Hell or Heaven set before the listener, with the way made so plain that fools need not err therein. And all this was addressed to the 'Saints', a concept which was peculiarly English. When Calvin mentions the 'Saints', it is nearly always the Saints in heaven to whom he refers. The radical continental reformers such as Thomas Muntzer or the Annabaptists use the words 'the elect' to describe the 'friends of God',[6] for the Saints to them were the faithful in glory. All these lived too near the Reformation in its Calvinist reaction to use the word 'Saints' in place of the 'elect', for there was too political a connotation about the word. But, this was not so to the English Puritans of the Jacobean age. The concept of God's election of some to salvation had become sophisticated in that the Church of England was theologically a Calvinist Church, and it might be said that all Englishmen were Elect, since all were in the Church. The concept had in other words, become inclusive rather than exclusive.[7] Even the actor, Nathan Field, could write to his minister in 1616 asking him not to preach against actors, as he, Nathan Field, was conscious of his election and was trying to make it effectual.[8] But how could an actor be one of the elect, since, as Preston says, 'the spirit breathes not in taverns nor playhouses, but in church assemblies' ![9] Consequently the word 'Saints' came into common

[6] Gordon Rupp, *Patterns of Reformation*, see Thomas Müntzer; *Golden Sceptre*, p. 545.

[7] Patrick Collinson, *The Elizabethan Puritan Movement*, p. 25.

[8] C. S. P. D. James I, 89/105 Field to Dr Sutton (1616).

[9] John Preston, *An Elegant and Lively Description* .., p. 35.

use among the Puritans to identify the elect, those who had been chosen by God to live the life of holiness in the sure certainty of their salvation. Theologically speaking the Elect were not identifiable, but the Saints were. They were the visible godly of the Old and New Testaments; the Christians of Corinth and Ephesus to whom St Paul wrote his letters. They were the faithful in an unbelieving and indifferent world. The Chasidim of the Psalms, which, for the Puritan as for the Monk, was the basic source of prayer and praise. In practical terms the Saints were the Christians who were trying, who were 'having a go' in living the godly life. They were particularly those who followed the Godly Preachers, and whether they were filled with apprehension of future judgement or buoyed up with hope of salvation, they were all conscious of having God's personal attention for good or ill. The concept of the 'Saints', pilgrims and warriors marching to Zion, identified the people who eventually became the Dissenters after the political collapse of the rule of the Saints on Cromwell's death, and there was in all the same consciousness of being the 'friends of God', the chosen people. Isaac Watts in the early years of the eighteenth century has this feeling in his hymns. After describing, for instance, the wonders of nature, the compassion of God in His dealings with humanity through nature, the force and skill of the creature in man and the animals, 'the piercing wit, the active limb', he can conclude that all these are too mean delights for God, and assert 'But saints are lovely in His sight'. Here is one of the authentic notes of Puritan spirituality, a people redeemed from the condemned world, who delight in God their Saviour, and who delights in them. So, says John Preston—answering the question 'would you have us to love none but the Saints?'—'It is true we ought to love others with a love of pittie. We should show abundance of this love to all mankind. But then there is the love of complacency and delight, and with this love we ought to love none but the Saints.'[10] Whilst the term 'Saints' was an English concept, it did not necessarily refer only to Englishmen, it also included those who belonged to 'the Kingdome of Grace abroad', to use a phrase of John Preston's. The 'Kingdom of Grace' is an

[10] John Preston, *The Breastplate of Faith and Love of Love* (1630), p. 102.

unprecise phrase, says Christopher Hill,[11] but precise enough to describe those of the religion, (another technical phrase of that time), that is the Reformed churches suffering under the Roman Catholic counter offensive. They, too, were the 'Saints' as indeed were the Piedmontese sufferers, for whom Cromwell intervened in 1655, and whose Latin Secretary, John Milton, while penning dispatches from his master to the Duke of Savoy, Cardinal Mazarin, or the Kings of Sweden and Denmark, asking for their intercession, could write the most passionate of all his sonnets '*Avenge O Lord, thy slaughtered Saints*'. The concept of 'Saints' gave a corporate identity to the elect, endowing them with a character and a visibility that marked them off from the world.

The first characteristic of the Saints, then, was that they were a people with an objective, an end for which to aim. Heaven was their destination, and though they already possessed the heavenly life, they knew that they had also to achieve it. They had been called by God in Christ to make this journey, they had been forgiven in Christ, they had been justified in Christ, they were sanctified in Christ, and they possessed the Keys of Heaven in Christ. They had an objective in a world which without this calling was a maze of defeated hopes and deceitful prizes. Of course, they had to be encouraged always to keep this end in view. 'God must be his end', says Preston, in describing the objective of the life of a Saint,[12] 'and nothing must stand in the way of achieving this end, for in due time the Saints would reign with Him in Glory.'[13] 'There is a certain Heaven which all Saints goe to',[14] says Preston addressing the Lawyers of Lincoln's Inn, and to the Parliament meeting at Oxford in 1625, 'we must mend our pace to Heaven'. The Saints must learn in spite of the satisfactions to be found in worldly things, that only Heaven contains true happiness. Such an objective demanded zeal, for Christ died 'that He might purifie unto himselfe a peculiar zealous people of good works'.[15] The Saints were encouraged in

[11] Christopher Hill, *Puritanism and Revolution* (Panther Ed.), p. 243.

[12] John Preston, *The Golden Sceptre,* (Of Seeking God's Face), p. 163.

[13] Ibid., The Churches Marriage, p. 59.

[14] Ibid., A New Creature, p. 396.

[15] John Preston, *The Golden Sceptre* (Sermon preached before Parliament), p. 268.

making Heaven their destination in that they having started could not fall from grace. Once they were in grace it was theirs for ever, for it was not something they earned, for who could earn God's forgiveness? It was not something for which they could bargain, for who could bargain with God? It was a gift of God to His chosen ones. Even sin in the Saint was not a falling from grace, indeed, 'grace gathers strength by it'.[16] It was very important for the Godly preachers to say something about sin in the Saints, because of their continual assertion that no Saint could fall from grace, and yet many fell into sin. So, Preston asserts that sin does not break the Covenant between God and the Saints[17] or daily failures weaken assurances.[18] Indeed, to refuse Christ when He is offered is worse than drunkenness or adultery.[19] It would be wrong to see these assertions as an expression of Antinomianism, because when all was said and done 'nothing troubles a holy man but sin'.[20] What differentiated the Saint from the un-regenerate was not that one fell into sin and the other did not, but that the Saint was 'troubled' when he sinned, but the un-regenerate was not. To him it was a way of life, as it were, and though he might feel the qualms of conscience he excused himself one way or another. A spiritual man on the other hand never excused himself, he never made 'peace with sin', he never said it is no use striving against sin. 'With every godly man, in every regenerate heart there is a Spring of Grace which works out anything that fouls it.'[21] An un-regenerate man on the other hand is like a pond of water, whatever falls in it lies there and fouls it. A Saint who had Heaven as his destination was bound to arrive, despite his failures and weaknesses.

The Saints were not alone on their journey, they were marching together, but more than that they had a supernatural travelling companion, the Holy Spirit. Though the Saints travelled together, each one had to be spiritually strong and

[16] John Preston, *The New Covenant* (Man's Uprightness. 8th Sermon), p. 4.

[17] Ibid., p. 215.

[18] John Preston, *The Golden Sceptre*, p. 122.

[19] Ibid., A Heavenly Treatise, p. 85.

[20] John Preston, *A Remedy Against Covetousness* (1632), p. 29.

[21] John Preston, *The Saint's Qualification* (1637), p. 267.

spiritual strength was dependent upon possessing the Holy Spirit. How to be certain that they possessed the Holy Spirit as the rule of life was of paramount importance to the Saint, and there is hardly a sermon of this period that does not emphasize this. It might be thought that there was something anarchic about this view, for 'The Spirit bloweth where it listeth' was a favourite text, and John Preston contrasted the wind of the Spirit with those sacramentarians who thought they had the 'wind in a bottle'. Yet, the Preachers were much concerned to emphasize the place of 'means' in the gift of the Spirit and by means they meant the means of Grace. 'You must use all meanes such as hearing the Word, receiving the Sacrament, Prayer, Meditation, Conferences, the Communion of Saints.'[22] Yet the Saint must not depend on the means without God, for the 'means' without God is like a pen without ink, a pipe without water, a scabbard without a sword. The Saint will not strengthen the inward man without God, but he must not depend on God without using the means of Grace. There was no anarchy of the Spirit about this. It was the rule of a disciplined, self-conscious, united people, receiving power from their Guide, the Holy Spirit, through the channel sanctified by long usage in the Church. The Saints were not a mob, but a disciplined army, who, Sunday by Sunday, received their marching orders, their guide lines for the journey from the Word, which was penned by the Spirit for their guidance, from the Spirit who inspired them daily to press on, and from the example of the Saints of old and their present companions. Christ their Captain and General had gone on ahead 'yet He hath left Guides to leade us in His stead; He hath left the Holy Ghost, the Spirit with us . . . you have the Spirit, the Word, and the Saints present and past to lead you'.[23]

The Saints on their journey to Heaven have the witness of the Spirit which is 'a divine expression of Christ to the Soul whereby a man is secretly assured without any argument or reason that He is his salvation'.[24] He must walk in the Spirit and be guided continually by the Holy Spirit, who will be to him as a 'Pilot

[22] Ibid., (Saint's Spiritual Strength), pp. 111–14.
[23] John Preston, *The Doctrine of Self-Denial*, pp. 102–4.
[24] John Preston, *The Golden Sceptre* (The Churches Marriage), p. 10.

with a ship, he will direct thy course and build up the Kingdom of Christ in thy heart'.[25]

On the journey to Heaven the Saints had to prepare themselves to enter Heaven, for only a particular kind of people could claim a title to Paradise: holy people who bore the image of Christ. 'Religion', says Richard Sibbes, 'is an art, not of great men, nor of mighty men, but of holy men.'[26] To be holy men, sanctified men, saints, was the objective of Puritan virtue, for only holy men could properly practise religion. Holiness or Sanctification, the Saint's passport to Heaven, is engendered in the soul by love. 'When the heart is prepared by humiliation and takes Christ', says Preston, 'love is wrought in the Soule, and love sanctifies; for sanctification is nothing else but a getting ourselves apart from common uses, and keeping of the heart close to God, making it peculiar to him, and this love makes us do'.[27] But sanctification was not just individualistic salvation. God might have saved men without sanctifying them, 'it had been no more than calling men at the hour of death'.[28] But God had called men to be holy. It is enough that He wills it and His will is sufficient to enforce it. It was the purpose for which Christ came to earth. 'If He had come only to save men, there had been no need of being new creatures, but He came also to 'purifie unto Himself a peculiar people, zealous of good works, and to destroy out of man the works of the devil, and to purchase to Himself an holy generation, a royal Priesthood.'[29] The Saint knew therefore that he belonged to a 'holy generation', a people set apart by God to demonstrate to the world the way to heaven by displaying the deeds of God in a fallen world. As Priest, Christ had reconciled God to them; they were given a chance, as it were, to inherit in Christ the promises of God. They alone in a condemned world were acceptable to God, but only because they were Christ's chosen and for no other reason. But Christ as Priest had not reconciled them to God. To do this He

[25] Ibid., p. 18.

[26] Richard Sibbes, *Saints Cordialls* (Sermon 22), p. 384.

[27] John Preston, *The Golden Sceptre* (Sermon, I, The New Creature), p. 293.

[28] Ibid., p. 298.

[29] Ibid., p. 299.

needed His two other offices of Prophet and King. 'For man stands out and will not know the way.'[30] Therefore, Christ in His Prophetic office and through His Surrogate the Holy Spirit, guides them into the way. But this is not all, because men were stubborn creatures inheriting all the pride and wickedness of the first Adam in which the Saints or chosen ones were no exception, Christ exercised His Kingly office to bring into subjection every thought to the obedience of His will.

In order to encourage the Saints to become holy, the Preachers preached and published innumerable sermons on the general theme of Guides to Godliness, and godliness was the possession of supernatural strength from the Holy Spirit. Each Saint had to desire and pray for this supernatural strength, for holiness consisted in the power to do God's will on earth as the angels do it in heaven. According to John Preston, in a sermon he published called *The Saint's Spiritual Strength*, there is a natural strength and a supernatural strength. Natural strength is when a man is naturally strong in his body or in the gifts of his mind. Included in the natural strength is often a moral strength, and with this a man may go very far, yet the Saint must not rest in this, but must remember that there are two sorts of supernatural strength; the first supernatural strength comes from the evil Spirit 'that is when Satan shall joyne with the spirit of man to do evil . . . with this spirit comes all the enemies of the Church strengthening withall'.[31] The supernatural strength for which the Saint must strive is that strength 'that comes from the sanctifying spirit whereby a Christian is able to do more than naturally he could do'. Preston defines the Saint's spiritual strength by saying that it is a general good disposition or right habit, temperament, or frame of mind, whereby the Saint is able to please God in all things. All Saints do not possess this strength in equal proportion, for some are subject to weakness. This weakness is not the weakness of man before conversion : that is not properly called weakness, but wickedness. 'Therefore know', he says, 'that the weakness he is speaking of is proper to a Christian and is of two sorts, weakness in knowledge, or the weakness of one who

[30] John Preston, *Golden Sceptre* (The New Creature), p. 299.

[31] John Preston, *Saint's Qualification* (The Saint's Spiritual Strength), p. 68.

was once strong, but is fallen sick so that he cannot use grace. They who are weak through lack of knowledge grow strong as the knowledge of Christ increases, the other sort grow weaker and must repent, and return to their first works.' His view is that man is born with certain natural powers, which of course vary from individual to individual, but these natural powers are the battle ground for the struggle between Satan and Christ. True to his scholastic reading, he held that grace does not destroy a corrupt nature, but elevates it by changing the will, and bestowing power to do good, and it is this power of grace which creates godliness in the Saints.

This objective of active holiness demanded a discipline as severe in its way as that of the monk, and to the Puritan Preachers the milieu of this discipline was the family. Puritan hagiology is full of descriptions of family discipline in prayer, bible exposition, sermon-tasting, attendance at the sacrament of the Lord's Supper, and good works: and good works were as important as any of the other demands. But the family was not in isolation, as it were, it was united with other like-minded people who pursued the same objective, people who were marching to heaven and developing the kind of disciplined spiritual life which would fit them for heaven. It was these families which supported the Prophesyings, Fasts, and Conferences, which were the media for the evangelical thrust of the Movement, and many a Lecturer unable to find maintenance in the Church, found a place as a private Chaplain or House Preacher in such homes.[32] After the Queen's death Puritanism under Buckingham's patronage became a kind of tolerated '*religio licita*', and the grass roots of the movement were to be found in these great Puritan families. Samuel Clarke, who published the lives of many Puritan Preachers, describes in his preface to *The Lives of Sundry Eminent Divines*, the Conferences he organized for the Saints. Clarke was born in 1599, and went to John Preston's College, Emmanuel, in 1616. He became the Lecturer in the parish of Thornton in the Wirral peninsula, where he stayed for five years, supported by the voluntary gifts of 'the godly' as he calls them. Once every three months he organized a Conference which drew

[32] Irvonwy Morgan, *The Godly Preachers of the Elizabethan Church*, pp. 215–17.

the Saints from all over the peninsula. These Conferences were held in the houses of the sympathetic Squires, and he describes how 'in the morning when they first met, the Master of the family began with prayer, then was the question to be conferred and read, and the younger members gave their answers, together with the proofs of Scripture for them.'[33] The older people then gave their answers, and after lunch they went on again with prayer and study until the early evening. Before he left, the Lecturer always gave them three questions to study in preparation for the next Conference. Well known Godly Preachers travelled long distances to preach at similar Conferences, and by such means there was built up a body of people who understood when they were addressed as 'Saints' that it was holiness which was their aim, a holiness which would entitle them to a place in heaven.

The Saint, however, was not just to be concerned with the salvation of his own soul, and its growth in grace and holiness, he had also an obligation to the un-regenerate multitude to offer them salvation in Christ. The Saint was bound to bear testimony to his own dealings with God, and, in the words of one of John Preston's converts, Thomas Goodwin, to tell such testimony as 'flags of mercy before a company of rebels to win them in'.[34] As the Saint marched to heaven in the army of the elect, he marched through rebel territory, full of people who had revolted against God, but to whom mercy was offered if they would believe. This obligation was undertaken not just that a man should stand up and be counted, as it were, but as part of the evangelical command to preach the Gospel, to every creature. In the reign of Queen Elizabeth the deprived Godly Preachers of Northampton, who had been deprived of their livings for organizing the Prophesyings in Northampton, appealed to the Queen for restitution on the grounds that 'the number of those who had been won by the Preachers was no small number'.[35] 'Flags of mercy' had been accepted by the rebels! All Puritan Conferences had this evangelical aim as part of their purpose, and saved Puritanism from congealing into introverted pietistic groups

[33] Samuel Clarke, *Lives of Sundry Eminent Divines*, Preface.
[34] Thomas Goodwin, *Works*, Vol. 5, *Life, by Thomas Goodwin Junior.*
[35] Seconde Parte of a Register I, p. 122.

bent only on their own edification. This urge to evangelism applies also to Puritan preaching for every sermon had to have its 'use' in bringing men to decision. Every sermon was a personal testimony in that the dynamic of the Preacher's appeal was grounded in his own experience, though the actual experience is very rarely mentioned. It was assumed that if the preacher appealed to the congregation 'to taste and see that the Lord is good', he himself had tasted and had seen that the Lord was good. Where these personal testimonies to God's dealings with man were to be seen was in the lives often prefixed to the volumes of printed sermons. These lives came to assume a biographical pattern in which the Preacher's own conversion was an essential ingredient: the jumping off place, as it were, which governed his future activity. It was these lives that Samuel Clarke assiduously collected for his publications. Sometimes these lives were revealed in the funeral sermons preached on the death of this or that Saint, sometimes they were first circulated in manuscript form after death, as was the case in Thomas Ball's *Life of John Preston*; and sometimes these lives were commissioned by Samuel Clarke himself. In the latter case lives were sometimes written by sons or friends who had been in the confidence of the subject, or extracted from diaries kept by the subject. But wherever the information came from Puritan lives all followed a similar biographical style, or were edited to conform to such a style by Clarke himself, in which the personal testimony of the subject to God's merciful dealings with him was always included. As 'flags of mercy' had been offered to and accepted by one rebel, such mercy was therefore available to others. Throughout the seventeenth century there was a growing interest in biography and Samuel Clarke and Thomas Fuller only did for the Church what Anthony Wood did for Oxford, and John Aubrey for a multitude of historical persons who could furnish an interesting anecdote! Puritan 'brief lives' were not however specifically history, but propaganda for the cause of righteousness. History was merely the stage on which the great drama of salvation was displayed and in its study a reader might well be surprised by grace.

The keeping of diaries, too, was a great aid to Puritan spirituality, for Puritan diaries were spiritual documents in which the soul in its struggles for holiness could be laid bare, much as in the Confessional. There its defeats in the battle with Satan were recorded, and its triumphs made an occasion for humble thanks to God. Such of the diaries as have survived,[36] have a rather 'counting house air' about them; a kind of spiritual book-keeping in which the Saint made up his account with God every day or every week. His blessings and triumphs went in on the receipts side and his defeats in the battle with Satan and sin on the expenses side. They were the places where man could accuse himself[37] before God and reflect on his peculiar temptations, reminding himself where grace might be found. These diaries were shared between friends for mutual edification and helped to build up a body of casuistical knowledge useful in what was called 'Conference' where a man sought another's help. Many Puritan Preachers became expert at what they called the comforting of 'afflicted consciences'. Richard Baxter systematized much of this casuistical knowledge in such works as his *Christian Directory*, as did Jeremy Taylor in his works. For the Saints and the Preachers such work, systematized or not, were not intellectual exercises, but part of an evangelical thrust on their journey to the Promised Land, whereby 'flags of mercy' were offered to rebellious souls.

When the Saint got to heaven that was the end of his journey. He no longer had any communication with the Saints below.[38] Indeed he did not know directly their struggles, and consequently could not be appealed to for help. The Saints would not have appreciated the remark attributed to Pope Paul VI. 'Why should we not pray to the Saints, they are our friends?' Only Christ knew of their battles and only He could help them through the power of the Holy Spirit. To pray to the Saints or to the Virgin was completely out of the range of their thought: such exercises were merely a device of Anti-Christ to turn men's minds away from Christ and His Gospel!

So the Saints when they came to the end of their earthly life marched into heaven in Christ's train to take possession of those heavenly mansions to which in His name they had a title.

36 William Haller, *The Rise of Puritanism*, ch. 3.

37 Irvonwy Morgan, *The Godly Preachers of the Elizabethan Church*, p. 171.

38 Richard Sibbes, *Saint's Cordialls*, p. 67 (but see Ch. 5, p. 71).

Thomas Goodwin describes this entry in his own way as John Bunyan did in his way. 'You heard before what welcome God gave Christ when He first arrived there, (in heaven after His ascension), and what He said to Him, and Christ said (as it were), to God : "I come not alone, I have much company, many of my brethren and followers to come after" (for it was the declared and avowed end of His coming to prepare a place for them). "I prayed when I was on earth that where I am they might be also" —John 17 : 24—"and now I am come hither, my train must come in too. I am not complete without them. If you receive me, you must receive them also and I am come to take up lodgings for them".' Thus the Captain of our salvation being 'made perfect, through suffering, and then 'crowned with glory and honour' in 'bringing many sons to glory', as Hebrews 2 : 10, of which Company He was the Captain, is brought in saying to God, Hebrews 2 : 13—"Behold I and the children God hath given me", he speaks it when brought to glory. "I am the Captain and they must follow me". "Where I am they must be. Lo, I am here and am not come alone, but to bring to glory all the children which thou hast given me"—"They shall be welcome", says God, "there is room enough for them, many mansions." So that we need not fear, nor say in our hearts doubting and despairing,— "Who shall ascend up to heaven for us, to bring us thither, Christ hath done it".'[39]

The final and definitive question for the Puritan as he thought of the journey of the Saints to heaven was 'Am I in the number?'[40] 'To believe the church', says William Perkins, 'is nothing else but to believe there is a company of the predestinate made one in Christ, and withal that we are in the number of them', and it is only these who enter the Kingdom of Heaven. There was no middle way. 'Either', says John Preston, 'I am in the number of those that are good, or those that are bad',[41] and it is incumbent on a man to know this and to be found among the righteous. 'Think seriously', he says, 'am I dead or alive? If dead, why then say, it is not in my power to quicken me, it is

[39] Thomas Goodwin, *Works*, Vol. 4, p. 51.

[40] Ian Breward, *William Perkins*, 'An Exposition of the Symbol', 301, p. 265.

[41] John Preston, *The New Covenant* (Foure Sermons), p. 24.

only in God to do it, and he doth this but in a few, how then shall I be in the number? Give yourselves no rest, know that it is God that breatheth, and then depend on Him.'[42] The number of the elect was God's concern, and when the Holy Spirit breathed on a man with the intention of conferring that holiness, without which no man can see God, that man was bound to learn even the hard way, how to co-operate with the inevitable.

[42] John Preston, *An Elegant and Lively Description*, p. 34.

INDEX

UNIVERSITY LIBRARY
NOTTINGHAM